TAKS Coach
English Language Arts

Grade 10

Sheila C. Crowell and Ellen D. Kolba
Executive Directors,
The Writers' Room Program

Acknowledgements

The authors wish to thank the following for permission to use their work:

Excerpts from Selma, Lord, Selma, by Frank Sikora. Copyright ©1979 by University of Alabama Press. Reprinted by permission of the publisher, University of Alabama Press

"Shining Moon" Copyright © 2002 by Jessica Wade. Reprinted by permission.

"The Race" Copyright © 2002 by David Fernandez. Reprinted by permission.

Selection from The Bluest Eye reprinted by permission of International Creative Management, Inc. Copyright © 1970 by Toni Morrison

The authors would also like to thank Marsha Kalman, Boris Kolba, Margi Sáraco, and Jay Wecht for their contributions to the writing of this book.

About the Authors

Sheila Crowell and Ellen Kolba are specialists in the teaching of writing and in preparing students for writing assessments. Their textbooks provide the affirmative support and scaffolding all students need to become better, more confident writers—thus, helping them improve their scores on state writing assessments. As staff developers and writing curriculum specialists, they train teachers to evaluate writing by first identifying and specifying the strengths in a draft and then using these strengths to prompt revision. To support the teaching of writing in their own school district in Montclair, New Jersey, they developed The Writers' Room Program, which trains volunteers from the community, students, and pre-service teachers to serve as writing coaches in elementary, middle, and high school Language Arts and English classes. Under their direction, The Writers' Room Program has been brought to other school districts in New Jersey, California, and Canada.

Our special thanks go to the many teachers in the state of Texas who, when we were first piloting our program, responded so positively to our methods. We remember especially the conferences and workshops in Arlington, Austin, Baytown, Corpus Christi, Dallas, Edinburg, Fort Worth, Houston, Humble, Irving, Pasadena, and San Antonio.

The TAKS English Language Arts Coach, Grade 10
43TX
ISBN# **1-58620-439-4**

Editor: Michael Sprague
Interior Design: Janet Yuen
Cover Design: Janet Yuen
Cover Photo: ©Arthur Tily/Telegraph Colour Library/Eight Teens in a Pyramid Formation

Educational Design 345 Hudson Street, New York, NY 10014-4502
©2003 Educational Design, a Division of Triumph Learning
A Haights Cross Communications company

Printed in the United States of America.

10 9 8 7 6 5 4 3 2 1

Table of Contents

NOTICE: Photocopying any part of this book is forbidden by law.

5

To the Student

The Texas Grade 10 English Language Arts test (TAKS) is principally based on a set of three pieces for you to read and analyze. This set of three pieces is referred to as a **triplet**. A triplet consists of the following:

- A literary (fictional) selection

- An informational (nonfiction)

- A one-page "viewing and representing piece"—that is, a piece that may contain some text but that is built around a visual representation of some kind. It may be an ad, a cartoon, a chart, a photograph, or something similar.

The pieces in the triplet are linked by a common theme. That is, they share a common idea or set of ideas. You will find that much of the test involves exploring the implications of this common theme and examining how the selections express it.

The test will test you in the following ways:

- **Multiple-Choice Items** test your understanding of the selections. Most refer to one selection only, but some ask you to compare or contrast more than one.

- **Open-Ended Items** ask you to write a short response to a question instead of having you choose an answer from a list. Like the multiple-choice items, they may refer to one selection only or to more than one.

- **A Written Composition** You will be asked to write an essay based on the theme of the triplet. You may write any kind of essay you wish, as long as it is in standard English prose.

The final section of the test is not necessarily based on the triplet. It is a test of your ability to revise and edit a sample student composition that contains a number of errors in sentence structure, usage, capitalization, punctuation, and spelling. A series of multiple-choice questions will ask you to identify and correct the errors.

This book will help you get ready for the test. It will review some of what you have learned about reading and writing, and it will show you some of the types of questions you can expect. When you have finished, you should be well prepared for the actual examination.

Good luck on the test!

UNIT 1
Reading

A. Basic Reading Strategies

Reading is the act of seeing markings on a page and turning them into words and thoughts in your mind. How well can you do this? That is what the **TAKS Grade 10 Language Arts** Test wants to find out.

In this part of *The TAKS Coach*, you will go over some of the basic reading strategies that are likely to be tested on the TAKS test. These should not be new to you. They are the same for everything you read on your own and in every course you take in school. The Coach will give you examples and selections for you to review and on which to practice. In addition, it will give you strategies and tips on how to approach test questions and make the most sense of what you are reading.

NOTICE: Photocopying any part of this book is forbidden by law.

7

1 Finding the Main Idea and Supporting Details

The most important idea that you are supposed to get from reading a block of text is called the **main idea**. Single paragraphs, sections of text, and whole informational articles—all will have a main idea.

Each main idea is supported by **details**. These supporting details are additional information that help to explain, clarify, or tell more about the main idea. However, supporting details are not the main idea itself.

If a multiple-choice test question asks you for a main idea, don't choose a supporting detail! You will often find answer choices that are statements contained in the selection, but whenever one of these is just a supporting detail, it's not the main idea.

In the following selection, you will be asked to find the main idea and supporting details in several paragraphs.

Example 1

Exoplanets

How many planets are there? Did you guess nine? Up to 1995, you would have been right. But starting in 1995, astronomers began to discover planets that spin around distant stars. Most of the newly discovered planets are giants, much larger than Earth, that orbit very close to their suns. Astronomers refer to them all as *exoplanets*, using the prefix *exo-*, meaning "outside"—that is, outside our own solar system. By 2002, the total number of known exoplanets was close to a hundred. But none of them resembled any planet in our solar system.

1   This paragraph is mostly about —

    A   the discovery of planets outside our solar system

    B   the nine planets in the solar system

    C   the prefix *exo-*, which means "outside"

    D   giant planets in our solar system

Choice **A** is correct. The **main idea** of this passage is contained in the fourth sentence: *But starting in 1995, astronomers began to discover planets that spin around distant stars.* All the other answer choices are **supporting details** or are statements that do not say what the paragraph says. Answer B is wrong because the paragraph *as a whole* is not about the nine planets in our solar system, but about the planets outside it. Answer C is also a detail. Answer D is wrong because the paragraph is about giant planets outside our solar system, not inside it.

Strategies and Tips
for Identifying Main Ideas and Details

1. You can often find a sentence in a paragraph that states the main idea. A sentence that states the main idea is called a topic sentence. (Not all paragraphs contain a topic sentence, however.)

    *   A topic sentence can appear anywhere in the paragraph.

    *   The most usual place for a topic sentences is the first sentence of the paragraph.

    *   If the topic sentence is used to sum up the contents of a paragraph, it may be placed last in the paragraph.

    *   Occasionally, the first sentence (or sentences) of the paragraph serves as an introduction, and the topic sentence follows it.

2. A heading or a title may tell you the main idea of a selection.

3. You can often get the main idea of a selection even if you don't understand every one of the details.

4. When a test question asks for a main idea, students sometimes choose a supporting detail from the passage instead. This usually happens because the detail is right there in the passage, and the student thinks it "looks right." Don't make this kind of mistake! Be sure to distinguish between the main idea and a detail that supports the main idea!

NOTICE: Photocopying any part of this book is forbidden by law.

9

Practice

Read the following additional sections of the selection and answer the questions.

> (*Special note to the reader:* The first paragraph below contains some strange names and numbers. Some readers stop reading when they come to material like this. Don't do what many students do and turn off! Keep reading, and try to get the general idea of the paragraph.)

Section 1

Many of the new exoplanets were discovered by an American team led by Geoffrey W. Marcy of the University of California at Berkeley, working with with Paul Butler of the Carnegie Institution of Washington, D.C. In 2002, Marcy and Butler's planet-hunting team discovered something new. It was a planet orbiting a star somewhat like our sun, a star in the constellation Cancer that is so far away you can barely see it with the naked eye. Astronomers call the star 55 Cancri A, and the new planet is called 55 Cancri d. (Star and planet names mean more to astronomers than they do to ordinary people.) Planet 55 Cancri d is a truly huge planet. It is somewhere between three and five times the mass of Jupiter, the largest planet in our own solar system. But it was not its size that made 55 Cancri d interesting to the astronomers—they already knew about other exoplanets that big. All the planets previously discovered are extremely close to their suns, and all move in strange, stretched-out orbits. What made 55 Cancri d interesting is that it is as far away from its star as Jupiter is from our sun, and it moves in an orbit shaped like Jupiter's. Until its discovery, we knew of no exoplanets that behaved anything like a planet in our own solar system.

1 This passage is mostly about —

   A a star that is so distant that we can barely see it

   B an exoplanet the size of Jupiter

   C an exoplanet with an orbit like Jupiter's

   D why a new planet was named 55 Cancri d

Section 2

How do astronomers like Marcy and Butler find new planets? Marcy and Butler use a telescope located at California's Lick Observatory. At any time, they are monitoring hundreds of stars with this telescope. But even with the Lick telescope, the astronomers can't actually see any exoplanets—they are too small for telescopes to pick out, and they are swallowed up in the glare of the stars they orbit. But the astronomers have devised a technique for discovering distant planets and determining important facts about them. They look for any shift in starlight— any wobble—that would suggest a planet orbiting and pulling the star. Then, from the amount of the shift, they can deduce both the size of the planet and its mass. But they have to measure this shift over a long period of time. Before discovering 55 Cancri d, Marcy and Butler had to make observations over a period of 15 years.

2 The main idea of this paragraph is that —

A astronomers find planets by measuring the wobble in their parent stars

B it took fifteen years to find 55 Cancri d

C Marcy and Butler are observing hundreds of stars

D Marcy and Butler use a telescope at Lick Observatory

Here is a longer passage. Read it and answer the questions.

Section 3

Planet 55 Cancri d was not the first planet of its star that Marcy and Butler discovered. Six years earlier they had found a planet a little less massive than Jupiter orbiting very close to the star 55 Cancri A. They believe that there may be a third big planet between the other two. Some astronomers wonder if there could even be an Earth-like planet located in the 55 Cancri A system. One astronomer has calculated that an Earth-sized planet could survive in a stable orbit between the two Jupiter-like planets. If such a planet exists, it may be able to support life. Whether or not it actually exists—or whether the tug of that third big planet would knock it out of a stable orbit—remains to be seen.

NOTICE: Photocopying any part of this book is forbidden by law.

11

One week after Marcy and Butler's announcement, a group of European astronomers announced that they had used similar methods to discover another planetary system that also has a planet similar to Jupiter. But the real prize will be the discovery of a planet like Earth. Astronomers know they need better techniques and instruments if they are to improve their chances of finding such a planet. One instrument that European astronomers have developed has the jaw-breaking name "High Accuracy Radial-Velocity Planetary Search Spectrograph," or HARPS. They will be using it from the European-run La Silla Observatory in Chile. They hope that HARPS will help them in the search for truly Earthlike exoplanets. However, actually finding one may be years away.

3a A good heading for the first paragraph would be —

    A A Planet Less Massive Than Jupiter

    B Marcy's Team Finds an Earthlike Planet

    C Stable and Unstable Orbits

    D More Planets Around 55 Cancri A

3b What is the main idea of the second paragraph?

    A HARPS is used in an observatory in Chile.

    B European astronomers discovered another solar system with a Jupiter-like planet.

    C HARPS is used by European astronomers.

    D Scientists are working on better equipment and techniques.

Answering an Open-Ended Question

One good way to test your ability to find a main idea is to write your own statement of the main idea. Since you won't have any answer choices to help you, read the passage. Then imagine that someone asks you what the main idea of the selection is. Think of your answer; then write the sentence on the line below.

Selection 4

Even more advanced than the HARPS system is the planned TPF—Terrestrial Planet Finder. TPF will be a space telescope that is specially designed to find new exoplanets, including ones as small as Earth. Not only will TPF be able to take pictures of such planets, it will measure their size, temperature, and orbits. It will even be able to find out whether a planet has an atmosphere capable of supporting life. Designs for TPF are scheduled for completion in 2006, and then the job of building it will start.

4   What is the main idea of selection 4?

_____

_____

Analyzing a Successful Response to an Open-Ended Question

Some questions may ask you to construct responses of your own that are longer than one sentence. Here is an example:

Summarize briefly the reading selection on exoplanets.

What do you need to do in order to answer this question?

- You need to base your answer on the whole selection, not just on one or two paragraphs.
- You need to write more than one sentence in response. (Notice how many lines are provided for the answer.)

The best way to learn to write a successful response of your own is to analyze the response of a good writer first.

Here is the way Alex answered the question above. Read what he wrote. Then answer the questions that follow to see what makes his answer so good.

Alex's Answer

> *In recent years, astronomers have been discovering huge planets outside our solar system. One example is a planet known as 55Cancri d, which is like Jupiter in its behavior. It takes many years of observation to identify one of these exoplanets, but astronomers hope someday to find one that resembles Earth. New instruments like HARPS (now in use in Chile) and TPF (which is being designed now) should help them do this.*

1   Alex's opening sentence states the topic. This lets the reader know what the paragraph is about. It also focuses the paragraph. (Notice that the details in the rest of the paragraph help develop this topic.)

Write the part of the opening sentence in which Alex states the topic.

_____

_____

2   Alex summarizes the reading selection by using relevant details from the whole article.

a. Write a detail that comes from section 1 of the article.

_____

_____

b. Write a detail that comes from section 2 of the article.

_____

_____

c. Find one other detail in Alex's answer, and identify the place it comes from.

_____

_____

3   Alex combines and connects details from more than one section of the article. For example, he combines details from sections 2 and 3 in his third sentence:

> It takes many years of observation to identify one of these exoplanets, but astronomers hope someday to find one that resembles Earth.

Write another sentence in which Alex combines and connects details from more than one section of the article.

_____

_____

2 Making Inferences and Drawing Conclusions

When you read, you must often use your own reasoning to supply missing information. This is called **making inferences** or **drawing conclusions**.

For example, suppose you read the following sports headline:

HITTERS OUTGUESSING PITCHERS THIS SEASON

You could figure out—**infer**—that the story was about baseball.

Similarly, if you read about someone who gave millions of dollars to an art museum, you might **conclude** that the person was both wealthy and interested in art.

A good part of successful reading, both on the TAKS test and in real life, depends on making correct inferences. In fact, much of the pleasure in reading comes in inferring something that the author has deliberately not told you. Practice making inferences and drawing conclusions in the following selection.

Example 1

> Sometimes what you don't say is more important than what is said. Isabella's friends were trying to convince her to go to an expensive, fancy restaurant for dinner. "No, I've got a big test tomorrow," she told them. When she walked away from them, she fingered the small change in her pocket, and tried to swallow through the lump in her throat.

1   From the passage, you can conclude that —

    A   Isabella doesn't really like her friends.

    B   Isabella doesn't have enough money for an expensive restaurant.

    C   She studies a lot.

    D   Isabella has a sore throat.

The answer is **B**, Isabella doesn't have enough money for an expensive restaurant. The other conclusions are not supported by the details in the passage or are contradicted by the passage.

NOTICE: Photocopying any part of this book is forbidden by law.

15

Strategies and Tips
for Making Inferences and Drawing Conclusions:

1 Be sure that your conclusion can logically be drawn from details in the selection.

2 Do not draw inferences that are too broad or too general.

Practice

Read the following paragraphs and answer the questions.

My Job As Music Critic

Selection 1

Back when I was a teenager, I used to dream about having a job where record companies would send me free music. I loved rock and roll, but couldn't afford to buy all the great albums that were being released. About fourteen years ago, my dream became a reality when I became a music critic. I sort of fell into this job. I started writing for a magazine, and was asked if I wanted to write a book review column. When the music column got too big for one critic, I asked if I could write about music, too. The problem was that he was being sent so much music, he couldn't keep up with it. The two of us together began to call publicists, record companies, and sometimes the artist themselves, requesting music and promotional material so that we could review their music. When you're with a new magazine, you've got to prove to the people you're requesting music from that you are a legitimate critic. That meant sending formal letters on letterhead, following up with telephone calls, sending issues of the magazine and anything else within reason that they ask for.

1 "When you're with a new magazine, you've got to prove to the people you're requesting music from that you are a legitimate critic," implies that

   A music is expensive.

   B some people pretend to be music critics.

   C you've got to prove to yourself that you really are a critic.

   D you've got to have a license to be a music critic.

Selection 2

Suddenly, we were bombarded with music, press releases, phone calls from people wanting to talk to us. This was more overwhelming than either of us imagined. We both had other jobs as well, so we spent many nights talking on the phone, and listening to music into the wee hours of the morning. There was one more component to our work. We had to go to concerts. Lots of them. Most of the concerts didn't start until eleven or twelve in the evening, and my "daytime" job started early—I usually had to be up at 4 AM to get to work on time. Often I wouldn't get more than a few hours sleep, and off I would go to my other job. Then my partner got hired as the music critic at a large Dallas paper, and I was left alone with twice the amount of work that I had before.

2   What is the **most** probable conclusion about what happened after the author's partner left to work for the Dallas newspaper?

    A   The author's workload increased.

    B   The newspaper quit running a music column.

    C   The author stopped writing about music.

    D   The author didn't go to as many concerts as before.

Selection 3

Every day I read every daily newspaper I could get my hands on, as well as music magazines and weeklies. I read good reviews and bad reviews and asked myself what made them that way. I asked myself why the critics and publication chose a particular album to review. I closely inspected the format of the reviews or essays I read. How did they start? Did they always follow the same format? How did they make their reviews interesting? I often read reviews of music I wouldn't think of buying until after I read the review.

I started out by modeling my reviews after some that I liked, eventually creating my own style. I also did a lot of research on everyone I wrote about. In addition to the publicity material I received, I'd listen to old albums, read past reviews, and check out newspaper clips about what was going on with them personally and professionally. Keeping up with all the changes was hard, but it was part of my job.

3a What inference can be made from paragraph 1?

    A The author would only listen to music if she liked a review.

    B Most of the reviews were not interesting.

    C There isn't just one style of writing a music review.

    D Usually critics like the music they choose to review.

3b What conclusion can you draw from these two paragraphs?

    A Reviewing music is always a fun job.

    B Writing music reviews involves constant research.

    C At times, the work was too much to handle.

    D Music criticism is not a very interesting career.

 **Now you try it. Look at the following paragraph. What conclusion can you draw? Write it on the line provided.**

Selection 4

Over the years I have written about music for many different magazines and newspapers. I stayed with one magazine for fourteen years, interviewed many artists, and learned most of all that I love to listen to music. I did sway people from their comfortable nests of listening to the same old music into other avenues and realms, and made some friends in the music business. Sometimes I thought I needed a shovel to get out of my front door with the amount of books and music that was stacked in my house. But hey… there are worse things in the world than being overwhelmed with music and books. I love it. It's what I always wanted.

4 What conclusion can you draw from this paragraph? Support your answer with evidence from the paragraph.

_____

_____

_____

Revising an Unsuccessful Response to an Open-Ended Question

In the last lesson in this unit, you took the first step in learning how to write a good response to an open-ended question. In this lesson, you will take the second step: you will revise a response that isn't good.

Here is another open-ended question about this reading selection. This one asks you to construct a longer response of your own.

What made the job of music critic so challenging for the author of this article? Support your answer with information from the selection.

Like the question you worked with in Unit 1, this question asks you to do the following:

- draw information from the whole selection
- write a short paragraph in response

Now look at the answer to this question that Tia wrote:

Tia's Answer

She dreamed about this job when she was a teenager. It turned out to be much harder to do than she thought because there was so much music. Also, she had to write a lot.

You can see, without even reading it, that Tia's answer is probably too short to be a successful response. Besides needing more details, what else does Tia's answer need in order to be successful?

Imagine that you have written the same response as Tia. Then answer the questions below in your own words to help you revise the response. Remember to use details from the reading selection in your improved response.

1   Have I stated the topic or main idea clearly? If not, how can I revise the first sentence?

    Write your revised opening sentence here.

    _____

    _____

2   How can I change sentence 2 to make my explanation clearer and more complete?

    Write your revised sentence here.

    _____

    _____

3   What other details can I add to sentence 3 to improve my response?

Write your revised sentence here.

_____

_____

4   What final detail can I provide in my response?

Write your new sentence here.

_____

_____

Responding to an Open-Ended Question on Your Own

Look once more at the article about being a music critic; then read the question below. This is an additional example of a question that asks you to construct a one-paragraph response of your own.

> **What advice would you give a friend who is dreaming of being a music critic? Support your answer with information from the selection.**

Remember to do the following:

- draw information from the whole selection.
- write a paragraph in response.

Use the suggestions below to help you plan your own response to this question.

1   Make sure that you state the main idea of your response in the opening sentence.

Write the main idea here.

_____

_____

2   Think about what details are most relevant and will provide the best support for your main idea. Find those details in the reading selection and list them here.

Supporting Detail 1:

_____

_____

Supporting Detail 2:

_____

_____

Supporting Detail 3:

_____

_____

3 Decide which idea or detail in the reading selection would make a good closing for your response.

Write that idea or detail here.

_____

_____

Now use the notes you made in your plan to write a four-sentence response to the question. Make sure that you do the following:

- Arrange your ideas in an order that makes sense—they don't need to be in the same order as in the reading selection.
- Combine some of your ideas, and be sure to write complete sentences.
- Use your own words—don't copy details directly from the reading selection.
- Stick to the point; avoid getting off the topic.

Write your answer here.

_____

_____

_____

_____

_____

_____

_____

_____

3 Summaries

The following chapter deals with one of the most difficult kinds of questions on a reading test— summary questions. This kind of question asks you to choose the best summary of a reading selection.

A summary is something like a main idea. But it is an expanded main idea, expressed in a two-or three-sentence paragraph. It contains information that a simple statement of the main idea does not. It may mention important details or topics discussed in the selection. It may also contain a concluding sentence that sums up the point, or "primary message," of the selection. You must watch out for both the details and the main message when you select the best summary from a list of four choices, and you may have to make use of your inference skills when you consider what the point of the selection is.

Since each of the four answer choices is a small paragraph, you can't just glance at them the way you could if they contained only a few words. You have to read each answer very carefully, paying close attention to how it differs from the others. Furthermore, the answers do not necessarily contain the exact words of the selection. You really have to use your head to choose the correct one.

REMEMBER: Summary questions are among the most difficult items on a test.

Read the following two-paragraph selection and select the best summary. (You'll work with it again in the following chapter.)

Example 1

Too Much TV

Sitting glued to the screen of a TV set has become a national obsession. We are turning into a culture of passive viewers, mere couch potatoes. Adults and children in America watch an average of four hours of TV daily. That might not sound like a lot, but when you add it up, it translates into nine years of TV watching by the time you're sixty-five years old. And when we are not watching TV programs, we are watching rented videos and DVDs. Yet, in the long run, all this is so forgettable. If we cut our TV watching down to an hour a day, how many people would really regret not having watched enough TV in their lifetime?

Gluing yourself to the front of the tube makes you less physically active, stifles your creativity, and stops you from thinking critically. TV advertisements lead you to buy too many things that you don't need. This is not only bad for your pocketbook, but for the environment as well, because eventually you throw away all that merchandise you didn't need in the first place. TV programs contain too much violence. Finally, TV viewing keeps us from reading as much as we once did. Americans rent about 6 million videos a day, compared to 3 million items checked out of a library on an average day.

1   Which of these is the best summary of the selection?

A   We shouldn't watch TV any more. It completely ruins our health, causes us to stop reading, and is the major cause of damage to the environment. Americans spend most of their lives in front of a TV set, and this has to stop.

B   We Americans watch too much TV—nine years by the time we are sixty-five—yet most of what we watch is not memorable. TV contains excessive violence; it stifles creativity; and it cuts into time we could be exercising, reading, or thinking; It even harms the environment by persuading us to buy things we don't need and eventually throw away.

C   TV is bad for us. It causes us buy too many products that we then throw away. This trash harms the environment.

D   We spend way too many hours watching TV. By the time we're sixty-five years old, we will have watched 9 years of television! Yet not many people will regret not having watched enough TV in their lifetime.

The best choice is **B**. It covers the main points of the selection. Choice A is inaccurate because it vastly exaggerates the message of the selection. Choice C only summarizes one point made in the second paragraph, and Choice D only summarizes the first paragraph.

Strategies and Tips
for Choosing the Best Summaries

1. Be sure that the summary you choose covers the important details or topics discussed in the selection.

2. Be sure that the summary covers all parts of the selection.

3. Be sure that the summary does not contain an opinion or a viewpoint that is at odds with what the selection says.

4. Above all—be especially careful with summary questions!

Practice

Identify the best summaries of the following selections by answering the multiple-choice questions. The first selection consists of two paragraphs. The second selection is a repeat of a selection you read in the previous chapter.

Selection 1

Title IX

In 1972 the U.S. government adopted a measure known as "Title IX." This federal statute forbids discrimination on the basis of sex in all schools that receive federal monies. While this applies to all school activities, it is especially relevant to girls' and boys' sports in high school. Before Title IX, there were few opportunities for girls to play sports. Most of the federal money spent on physical education went to boys' sports. In addition to improving girls' sports opportunities, Title IX has proven to be very important for their education as well. Girls who are encouraged to play sports in school have a higher graduation rate than those that don't play sports at all. They are also less likely to get involved in drugs. Playing sports raises their self-esteem. Some female athletes receive athletic scholarships for college, opening up even more opportunities for them.

Title IX has affected Texas as well as the rest of the country. Let's look at some Texas women in sports. Sheryl Swoopes, a WNBA (Women's National Basketball Association) player, born in Brownfield, Texas, was the first woman to have her own Nike basketball shoe named after her. She was named the WNBA Player of the Year and Defensive Player of the Year partly because she led the WNBA with an average of 20.7 points per game. Texas Tech's head coach, Martha Sharp—probably one of the best woman's basketball coaches in the country—has taken her Lady Raiders team to an unbelievable fourteen NCAA Tournament appearances, including 12 in a row. Flo Hyman, at 6'5", is considered to be the best woman's volleyball player in history. After attending the University of Houston, she continued to compete, playing for two American Olympics volleyball teams. Flo earned the nickname "Clutchman" for an arm swing that produced a 110-mph spike. Title IX helped all these women to make sports history.

1 Which of these is the best summary for this selection?

A Title IX has been very important for girls' education. Before 1972, there weren't as many opportunities for girls to play sports as there were for boys. Now we know that girls who play sports do better in school, are eligible for college scholarships, and feel better about themselves.

B Three female athletes have had terrific careers and achievements. Sheryl Swoopes is a terrific WNBA player. Martha Sharp coaches Texas Tech's Lady Raiders. Flo Hyman is considered to be the best volleyball player in history. There are more athletes training right now, who might turn out to be the next Swoopes, Hyman, or Sharp.

C Before Title IX was passed in 1972, more money was given for boys sports. Not much has changed since then, except that Sheryl Swoopes, Flo Hyman and Martha Sharp have had great careers. Swoopes is a WNBA player, Sharp is known for coaching college Woman's Basketball and Flo Hyman is probably the best volleyball player in history.

D Title IX, adopted in 1972, required all schools that received federal money to give equal opportunities to girls as well as boys in all school activities. This sparked a jump in girls' sports opportunities, which proved to benefit their education as well. In Texas it helped make possible the careers of WNBA star Sheryl Swoopes, champion volleyball player Flo Hyman, and the outstanding Lady Raiders basketball team.

Selection 2

My Job As Music Critic

Back when I was a teenager, I used to dream about having a job where record companies would send me free music. I loved rock and roll, but couldn't afford to buy all the great albums that were being released. About fourteen years ago, my dream became a reality when I became a music critic. I sort of fell into this job. I started writing for a magazine, and was asked if I wanted to write a book review column. When the music column got too big for one critic, I asked if I could write about music, too. The problem was that he was being sent so much music, he couldn't keep up with it. The two of us together began to call publicists, record companies, and sometimes the artist themselves, requesting music and promotional material so that we could review their music. When you're with a new magazine, you've got to prove to the people you're requesting music from that you are a legitimate critic. That meant sending formal letters on letterhead, following up with telephone calls, sending issues of the magazine and anything else within reason that they ask for.

Suddenly, we were bombarded with music, press releases, phone calls from people wanting to talk to us. This was more overwhelming than either of us imagined. We both had other jobs as well, so we spent many nights talking on the phone, and listening to music into the wee hours of the morning. There was one more component to our work. We had to go to concerts. Lots of them. Most of the concerts didn't start until eleven or twelve in the evening and my "daytime" job started early—I usually had to be up at 4 AM to get to work on time. Often I wouldn't get more than a few hours sleep and off I would go to my other job. Then my partner got hired as the music critic at a large Dallas paper, and I was left alone with twice the amount of work than I had before.

Every day I read every daily newspaper I could get my hands on, as well as music magazines and weeklies. I read good reviews and bad reviews and asked myself what made them that way. I asked myself why the critics and publication chose a particular album to review. I closely inspected the format of the reviews or essays I read. How did they start? Did they always follow the same format? How did they make their reviews interesting? I often read reviews of music I wouldn't think of buying until after I read the review.

I started out by modeling my reviews after some that I liked, eventually creating my own style. I also did a lot of research for everyone I wrote about. In addition to the publicity material I received, I'd listen to old albums, read past reviews, and newspaper clips about what was going on with them personally and professionally. Keeping up with all the changes was hard, but it was part of my job.

Over the years I have written about music for many different magazines and newspapers. I stayed with one magazine for fourteen years, interviewed many artists, and learned most of all that I love to listen to music. I did sway people from their comfortable nests of listening to the same old music into other avenues and realms, and made some friends in the music business. Sometimes I thought I needed a shovel to get out of my front door with the amount of books and music that was stacked in my house. But hey… there are worse things in the world than being overwhelmed with music and books. I love it. It's what I always wanted.

2   Which of these is the best summary for the selection?

A   As soon as the opportunity crossed the writer's path, she asked to become a music critic. She had no idea how much music she was actually going to receive from record companies and public relations firms. Her dream quickly became a nightmare, as she tried to make her way through all that music piled around her.

B   The writer didn't have the expertise to write about music, and she and her partner had to stay on the publicity lists they worked so hard to get on. She learned to write about music by reading lots of music reviews from every magazine and newspaper she could get her hands on. She read both "good and bad reviews" and tried to determine what made them good or bad in her mind. She mimicked the ones she liked, and after awhile she was developing her own style. This took a great deal of work and research.

C   The writer's reason to become a music critic was because she liked getting a lot of free music and wanted to influence people's buying habits. Many people are critical of music they haven't really listened to at all. Other people don't know about the new music that is being released. She wanted to make a difference, and she succeeded.

D   A fourteen-year dream came true when the writer was accepted as a music critic for a magazine. Working at first with a partner, and later by herself, she dealt with music promotions, concert-going, and reviewing music, all while holding down a different day job. She sharpened her skills by reading other music reviews, at first imitating them and later developing a style of her own. She loves what she does, interviewing artists, listening to the music she loves, and turning readers on to music they might otherwise never have heard.

4 Identifying Text Structures and Patterns

Informational text can be organized in a number of ways. The kind of organization—what we call the text structure—varies with the author's purpose. For example, a writer who wants to compare and contrast two events will use a different organizational pattern from one used by the writer who wants to explain what caused something to happen. Recognizing the text structure can help you understand the author's purpose.

In order to figure out what kind of organizational pattern a writer has used, think first about the writer's purpose. Ask yourself questions like the ones below, and look for additional key words like those in boldface italic type.

- **Comparison and Contrast.** Is the writer trying to show what people, objects, or events have in common and how they are different from each other?

  similarities   differences   on one hand   on the other hand

- **Question and Answer.** Is the writer answering one or more questions in order to provide information on a topic?

  What are . . . ?   What do . . . ?

- **Problem-Solution.** Is the writer proposing solutions to a problem?

  solve . . .   deal with . . .   overcome . . .   the problem

- **Chronological.** Is the writer explaining events in a time sequence, from first to last?

  to begin   then   next   finally

- **Persuasion.** Is the writer trying to convince the readers to adopt a particular point of view or to take a specific action?

  I think   I agree   I disagree   In my opinion

- **Cause-Effect.** Is the writer explaining what causes specific things to happen or what happens as a result of particular events?

  because   as a result   the reason that

Example 1

Certain kinds of text structures can be represented by a diagram. See if you can identify the organizational pattern represented by this diagram:

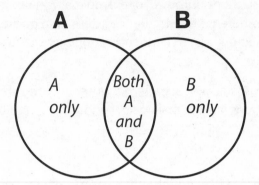

1   Which kind of organizational pattern is represented by this diagram?

   A   problem-solution

   B   persuasion

   C   comparison and contrast

   D   cause-effect

The correct choice is choice **C**—comparison and contrast. Comparison and contrast text explains how two things are alike and how they are different. A text like this often has a paragraph that explains how the two things—A and B—are alike. It also has a paragraph that explains the ways in which A is special or unique and a paragraph that explains the ways in which B is special or unique. The diagram—called a **Venn diagram** after its inventor—shows this.

Example 2

Too Much TV

Sitting glued to the screen of a TV set has become a national obsession. We are turning into a culture of passive viewers, mere couch potatoes. Adults and children in America watch an average of four hours of TV daily. That might not sound like a lot, but when you add it up, it translates into nine years of TV watching by the time you're sixty-five years old. And when we are not watching TV programs, we are watching rented videos and DVDs. Yet, in the long run, all this is so forgettable. If we cut our TV watching down to an hour a day, how many people would really regret not having watched enough TV in their lifetime?

Gluing yourself to the front of the tube makes you less physically active, stifles your creativity, and stops you from thinking critically. TV advertisements lead you to buy too many things that you don't need. This is not only bad for your pocketbook, but for the environment as well, because eventually you throw away all that merchandise you didn't need in the first place. TV programs contain too much violence. Finally, TV viewing keeps us from not reading as much as we once did. Americans rent about 6 million videos a day, compared to 3 million items checked out of a library on an average day.

2   What method of organization does the author use in this passage?

A   question-answer

B   comparison and contrast

C   problem-solution

D   cause-effect

This passage is written in the cause-effect format, which is choice **D**. It explains how much TV the average American watches. Then they go on to explain that watching too much TV can cause physically problems and effect your thinking processes.

Example 3

Zero Tolerance for Violence

After several violent incidents at schools across the country, our school principal has instituted a "zero tolerance" policy. "Zero tolerance" means that there are no excuses. In our school, if you are caught fighting, threatening to fight someone, or even arguing in school, you can be suspended or expelled depending on how severe the incident is. There are many times when students are fighting. While I think it is a very good idea to address this issue, there are more effective ways to deal with violent behavior.

One way to solve this problem would be to hold regular sharing circle sessions. This can be done in an extended homeroom period at the beginning of the day. These sessions are helpful for students because they can talk out their problems, or voice their concerns before they become too overwhelming. I have participated in these sharing circles before, and find them very helpful. Some people think that they're stupid and not worth their time, but even after one session, you can see the difference. It got to the point where students began to request them, even when they weren't scheduled.

3   What method of organization does the author use in this passage?

    A   question-answer

    B   comparison and contrast

    C   problem-solution

    D   cause-effect

This is a problem-solution passage. The answer is **C**. The first paragraph states the problem, violence in school. The second paragraph offers one solution, sharing circles. The other choices are incorrect.

Strategies and Tips
for Identifying Text Structures and Patterns

The main strategies that apply to this lesson are laid out at the beginning of the lesson. Learn them, and apply them whenever you read a selection.

Practice

Read each of the following selections and identify the organizational pattern of the text by answering the multiple-choice question at the end.

Selection 1

E-Mail

We have become so used to sending and receiving e-mail, but not many people know how e-mail is transmitted. First, as you know, you have to write a message to someone on your computer and click on the send button. Then things get complicated. Your e-mail "client," like AOL or Yahoo, connects to a SMTP "server" that takes care of outgoing mail. Next, the SMTP server and the e-mail client have a computer conversation. The e-mail client tells the SMTP server who the message is from, who the message is to, and what the message is. Then the server breaks the message into two parts: the recipient's name and the domain name.

At this point, the DNS takes over and asks the SMTP server for some addresses. The message gets handed over to the POP3 server, which handles incoming mail. The message is placed in the mailbox where it was addressed to go to. Finally, the person who owns that account, logs in with their account name and password and picks up the message.

(**Hint:** Unless you are a computer expert, you may not understand all the terms in this selection. But you should be able to answer the question at the end anyway.)

1   Which organizational pattern best describes the structure of this passage?

    A   question-answer

    B   comparison and contrast

    C   problem solution

    D   chronological

Selection 2

Pitching or Dancing?

Fifteen-year-old Imani is a locally-sought-after fast-pitch softball player and an excellent dancer. I asked her what would she do if she had to choose between dancing and pitching. At first she told me about some differences between dancing and pitching. For instance, when she's pitching she can only see the catcher and the batter. In dance she has to concentrate on the whole audience. When she pitches, she might get a little nervous, but when she dances she gets lots of butterflies in her stomach. Dancing makes her feel joyous, but pitching makes her think really hard.

Ultimately, Imani said she couldn't choose between dancing and pitching, because she likes them both. First of all, she is good at both. Second, some of her friends both dance and play sports. Sometimes her friends come to her games and dance performances. Finally, because she's been playing softball since she was 6 and dancing since she was 4, it would be hard for her to choose between softball or dance. They are both a big part of her life.

2 How is this passage organized?

    A   question-answer

    B   comparison and contrast

    C   problem-solution

    D   chronological

Selection 3

Raising the Passing Grade

Would it be a good idea to raise passing grades in high school from a "D" to a "C?" Recently, this has become a hot topic of discussion. After all, everyone is concerned with raising student achievement levels. After considering many different aspects of this issue, I have come up with a response. I don't believe passing grades should be raised to a "C."

First of all, focusing on grades will leave less time to learn without constantly being judged. Sometimes it is easier to work on a project without having to worry about what grade you're going to get, or if you will pass. Besides, not everything we do in life is graded. Visual artists don't get a grade on a painting they're working on, but if someone likes it they will buy it. While the artist is painting, hopefully they're only worried about creating their artwork, so they'll do the best job they can.

Teachers will be overburdened and frustrated trying to force students to pass with a "C" average. Teachers do a lot during the course of a school day already. I know my teachers are always complaining that they don't have enough time to grade our tests, or find interesting assignments for us to work on. Too much of their energy is already focused on grades. They might have to work harder to get their students to pass with a "C," but nobody will have a good time doing it.

3 What organizational format was used in this selection?

    A question-answer

    B cause-effect

    C problem-solution

    D chronological

Selection 4

Nutrition Classes

The local Board of Education is thinking of requiring a nutrition class, "The Way to Better Health," to supplement our Family Life class. Topics for study and discussion would include the importance of fitness, maintaining a healthy body image, and food and personal health. In addition there will be individual meetings with a nutritionist. I am glad someone is finally taking our health so seriously. I do not oppose this idea, I think it is a very good one.

Many of the students in high school have become very unhealthy. We are stressed out because of all the work we have to do both during the day and after-school. Our lunches are over too quickly (it's not good to eat too fast), and if you buy lunch the food is terrible. It's difficult for our parents to help us choose the right foods for lunch when we're eating at 10:30 in the morning! Perhaps if we made students more aware of what the food was doing to our bodies, how it was making us more tired and less productive, then we could work toward better nutrition.

It would be a wonderful idea to have a private nutritionist speak with each student directly and also to create a personal fitness plan. First of all, no one wants to admit their eating problems, especially if they're overweight, in front of other students. This way you could be honest with the nutritionist and get the help you need. The other part of the course that is so important is fitness. It's hard to motivate yourself to exercise when you're so overworked, but it is a skill we need to learn now. When I was younger, I exercised all the time, but I can't seem to find the time, now. I would suggest that the teachers bring in guests who are physically fit, like athletes and dancers to talk about their experience of exercising.

4   How did the author organize this selection?

A   question-answer

B   cause-effect

C   persuasive

D   chronological

5 Finding Cause and Effect

When you read, it is important to notice why things happen.

A **cause** is the reason that something happens. An **effect** is what happens as a result of that cause.

Cause-and-effect relationships are often signaled by certain words and phrases, such as because, since, as a result, so, therefore, consequently, or due to. Sometimes causes and effects happen in a chain. The effect of one cause becomes the cause of the next effect.

| CAUSE | → | EFFECT | = | CAUSE | → | EFFECT | = | CAUSE | → | EFFECT |

Read the following passage and answer the question that follows.

Example 1

Writing with Strings

Throughout history, people have always wanted to speak to each other over great distances. Today we have e-mail and chat rooms, phones and faxes and Fed-Ex, UPS and the good old U.S. Post Office. But before airplanes, trucks, telephone wires, and electronic signals carried our messages, they were transmitted via horses, runners, and even smoke signals.

Some of the most ingenious methods of communication were used by Native Americans. The Native American use of smoke signals is well known. But the people of the Pre-Columbian Inca Empire of Peru had an even more unusual method of recording and transmitting information. The Incas did not have a formal writing system. Instead, they used strings with elaborate colored fringes and rows of knots, called *quipu*, to record data. (The word *quipu* actually means "account.") We do not know all the details of the system, but apparently one of the most important functions of the *quipu* was to carry the numerical data—census figures, crop records, lists of warehouse contents, and the like—that the Inca bureaucrats needed to keep their 2000-mile-long empire running. The Incas established an elaborate messenger service using special runners carrying *quipu*. They would send runners racing back and forth on the High Inca's business over the excellent stone highways that they built throughout their empire.

Sadly, there are only about 400 surviving *quipu* in the world today. The Spanish conquerors in 1583 burned the archives of Inca *quipu*. All of the ones we have now have been dug out of human graves.

1   What was the principal effect of the Inca *quipu* system?

    A   The Incas were able to build good roads.

    B   The Incas were able to keep track of what was going on in their empire.

    C   The Spanish were able to beat the Incas.

    D   The Spanish burned the library of *quipu*.

The correct answer is **B**, The Inca bureaucrats used the information on the quipus to keep track of what was going on in the empire. The other answers are all true statements, but none of them is an effect of the quipu system.

Strategies and Tips
for Identifying Causes and Effects

Remember that the **cause** is why something happens. The **effect** is what happens because of it.

If a test question asks about a cause or an effect, don't choose just any statement that happens to be true. The statement must also be an answer to the question about cause or effect!

Practice

Read the following selections and answer the questions.

Section 1

The Pony Express

In the early days of the Old West, the United States needed a good way to take mail back and forth across nearly two thousand miles of country. Eastern Railroads ran only as far west as Missouri. A letter to the West Coast might have to go via a ship sailing around the tip of South America!

In 1860 a company called The Central Overland California and Pike's Peak Express Company (or C.O.C. & P.P. for short) came up with an answer—a system of horseback relay riders to carry the mail between Missouri and San Francisco. The company declared that it could deliver the mail 1,966 miles between Missouri and California, in less than 10 days.

1   One effect of the mail system in use before the Pony Express was —

   A   A letter from Virginia to San Francisco took several months to deliver

   B   Letters could be delivered in ten days from coast to coast

   C   Letters could not be delivered to California

   D   Railroad lines stopped in Missouri

Section 2

The company put out wanted ads for the first letter carriers: "Wanted—young, skinny, wiry fellows, not over 20. Must be expert riders, and are willing to risk their lives for the job. Orphans preferred. Wages twenty-five dollars a week." Even in those days it wasn't a lot of money. The employees joked grimly that the initials C.C.O. P.P stood for "clean out of cash and poor pay."

Nevertheless, the ads attracted riders. Boys a lot younger than 20 joined up. One of the most famous Pony Express riders— he was only 14 at the time—was the legendary cowboy Buffalo Bill. The youngest was 11-year-old Bronco Charlie Miller.

2   Why did the advertisement for Pony Express Riders prefer orphans?

    A   Not many riders came back alive.

    B   They knew that orphans would accept $25 a week salary.

    C   They preferred riders to have no attachments to families, so that they would be more willing to take risks.

    D   They would spend too much time away from home.

Section 3

Instead of one rider carrying the mail across the various states, company planners decided that each individual rider would travel 100 miles, stopping only to switch horses every ten to twenty miles. Then, after 75 to 100 miles, another rider would take his place. Eventually, there were 190 stations on the Pony Express trail. They used around 80 riders and between 400 and 500 horses. Each stretch could be fraught with hazards. For instance, riders might have to fight off—or outride—robbers, because they were often carrying valuables like gold, jewelry, and money. Bad weather conditions could also make trips perilous.

The Pony Express served another important function—keeping people informed about what was going on in the rest of the country, like Abraham Lincoln's election in 1860 and the outbreak of the Civil War. It seems strange to us now, but at that time you could live in the Southwest or West, have a war going on in your own country, and not know about it. A war could end without your knowing it, too. The American Civil War ended with General Lee's Confederate soldiers surrendering on April 9, 1865, but the news did not reach Texas for over a month. The last Civil War battle was fought on Palmito Hill, Texas, on May 12th and 13th. Not until May 18 did Texas know that the war was over.

3a   What caused the Pony Express's success?

    A   They relied on a few specially trained riders.

    B   They picked only the very fastest horses.

    C   They constantly replaced horses and riders.

    D   They didn't run during bad weather.

3b Which event in the second paragraph above was partly caused by poor communications?

    A General Lee's surrender.

    B the Battle of Palmito Hill.

    C the election of Abraham Lincoln.

    D the start of the American Civil war

Selection 4

Ironically, less than two years after the Pony Express began, it was closed down. It was losing large amounts of money. But even more important, an electric telegraph line had finally been strung across the country. Profitable or not, the Pony Express was no longer necessary. But, in the short time the Pony Express was in existence, its riders carried over 34,000 pieces of mail over 650,000 miles. Only one sack of mail was ever lost.

4 Why do you think people preferred the electric telegraph to the Pony Express?

_____

_____

_____

_____

_____

_____

_____

6 Comparison and Contrast

In your reading, you will often come across passages that clarify or explain things by showing how they are alike or different. Comparison shows how two things are alike. Contrast shows how they are different.

Comparing and contrasting are often signaled by words and phrases such as *like, unlike, similarly, instead, in the same way, on the other hand, both, however,* and *on the contrary*. Single paragraphs, longer passages, and whole texts may be organized by comparison and contrast.

Read the following passage and answer the question.

Example 1

The Migrating Monarchs

You probably know that the official state flower of Texas is the bluebonnet, and the state bird is the mockingbird. But did you know that Texas also has an official state insect? In 1995 the Texas legislature bestowed that honor on the monarch butterfly. It was chosen because every spring and fall millions of the butterflies appear in the sky over Texas. There are two different areas to see them, west-central Texas and the Texas coastal region.

This strange explosion of butterflies takes place because monarch butterflies in the United States and Canada do not hibernate during the winter, as other butterflies do. Instead, they migrate thousands of miles south to a warmer climate. Monarchs are the only butterflies that do this. Whereas most other butterflies lay eggs in the fall and die, the monarchs head for Mexico—and pass over Texas on their way to a relaxing, sunny winter. In Mexico they come together in colonies high in the mountains. A colony can have up to 6 million butterflies per acre, and colonies can fill up to 10 acres. That's 60 million monarch butterflies at one site! In late winter they mate, and shortly afterwards they start returning north again to lay their eggs.

1a The behavior of the monarch butterflies in this passage is most like —

  A certain birds

  B certain farm animals

  C certain reptiles

  D certain spiders

The correct answer is **A**. Monarchs migrate south in the fall and return north in the spring, and so do many kinds of birds. The other creatures do not migrate this way.

> **1b** One thing that makes monarchs different from other butterflies is that —
>
> **A** monarchs spend the winter in Texas
>
> **B** monarchs lay eggs in the fall
>
> **C** most other butterflies die in the fall
>
> **D** most other butterflies migrate in the fall

Here the correct answer is **C**. Most other butterflies die in the fall, but monarchs do not. They migrate south in the fall and return north in the spring. A is wrong because monarch butterflies spend the winter in Mexico, not Texas. B is wrong because other butterflies, but not monarchs, lay fall eggs. D is wrong because monarchs, but not most other butterflies, undertake long-distance migrations.

Strategies and Tips
for Identifying Comparison and Contrast

1. When looking for **similarities** between two things, eliminate answer choices that are true of only one or that are true of neither.

2. When looking for **differences** between two things, eliminate answer choices that are true of both or that are true of neither.

Practice

Read the following paragraphs and answer the questions.

Section 1

Many species of butterflies travel short distances in search of food; when the food is better for the butterflies to eat, they return to their original locations. This is not real migration, however. About 200 kinds of butterflies and moths are true long-distance migrators. However, except for monarchs, the migrants never return. The insects that fly back the following year are the children or grandchildren of the original migrants. Only monarchs make the journey in both directions. The monarch butterflies that fly north in the spring are the same ones that went south the previous fall. And they can travel up to three thousand miles, which is farther than any other butterfly.

1   How do the migration patterns of monarch butterflies different from those of other butterflies?

    A   Other butterflies do not migrate at all.

    B   Monarchs migrate from north to south, while other butterflies migrate from east to west.

    C   Monarchs are true migrants, while other butterflies travel only short distances in search of food.

    D   Only monarchs make a round trip.

Section 2

Monarch butterflies live on milkweed; wherever you find milkweed, you'll find the butterflies. And since milkweed is so common, you'll find monarch butterflies all over the United States during the summer months. Then, as the milkweed goes to seed in late summer, they prepare for their great migration. Mexico is the destination for butterflies from east of the Rocky Mountains. Those from the central part of the country, like Minnesota, reach Texas first. They pass through central Texas in early and mid-October. A second wave comes from eastern states like Massachusetts, They reach the Gulf Coast in mid- to late October. West of the Rocky Mountains, the monarchs migrate to wintering places along the California Coast.

2   Contrast the migration pattern of monarch butterflies born in Minnesota with those born in Oregon.

   A   Oregon butterflies migrate several months earlier than those born in Minnesota.

   B   Oregon butterflies migrate to California; Minnesota butterflies migrate to Mexico.

   C   Oregon butterflies do not migrate at all.

   D   Oregon butterflies do not migrate back north, while Minnesota butterflies do.

Section 3

How long does a monarch butterfly live? The answer depends a lot on when it was born. The generation of monarchs that travels to Mexico in the fall and back to the United States in the spring lives about eight to nine months. The next three or four generations—ones that are born in the United States or Canada in the spring and summer—can live as short a life as four to six weeks. The last summer generation, however, starts the cycle over again. But even the summer-generation monarchs live longer than many other kinds of butterfly. Most other species usually only live one to two weeks in their adult stage, although there are some exceptions. Some butterflies live as few as three days.

3   Which has the longer natural life span—a monarch butterfly born in early June or one born in early September?

   A   The butterfly born in June will probably live longer.

   B   The butterfly born in September will probably live longer.

   C   They both have about the same natural life span.

   D   You can't tell—the month of their birth has nothing to do with their natural life span.

Section 4

Animals and insects—not just monarch butterflies alone—migrate because they need to adapt to a changing environment in order to survive. They migrate to follow their food, avoid potentially harmful weather, or to avoid predators. Migration patterns of animals and insects usually follow the exact same routes every year, whether they are birds flying long distances, whales swimming halfway across the world, or insects flying three thousand miles, as the monarch butterflies do. Of course, most animals and insects adapt to their environment without migrating. During winter, butterfly caterpillars may dehydrate themselves so that the water in their tiny bodies doesn't freeze, which would eventually kill them. Or, they adapt their life cycles, so that they are in the egg or larval stages in the coldest months. Yet the monarch butterfly migrates. Why doesn't it do what other butterflies do? Scientists are still puzzled by this tiny, amazing insect.

4   What are some similarities between why animals and insects migrate?

_____

_____

_____

_____

_____

_____

_____

7 Vocabulary 1: Using Context Clues

In your reading, you will often run into words whose meaning you do not know. Fortunately, the words just before or after the unfamiliar word often give you clues to its meaning. These clues—hints from the surrounding text—are called **context clues**. In your everyday reading as well as on a test, you should look for context clues whenever you come across a word you don't know. For example, see if you can guess at the meaning of elixir in the following passage:

> In our modern era, medicines must be scientifically tested before they can be sold to the public. But a hundred years ago, your great-grandmother might have relied on some bottled *elixir* with a name like "Dr. Whuppo's Patented Cure-All Tonic" to get rid of her headaches.

The context clues should tell you that in this selection, an *elixir* is a liquid claiming to have curative properties.

Sometimes the context clues appear in a separate sentence:

> It is difficult to live with a *hypochondriac*. People who imagine they are always sick cannot be convinced that they are perfectly healthy, and that their symptoms are either normal or imaginary.

You may also find unfamiliar words that are not defined at all, but the context will still give you a clue to their meaning. For example,

> Nobody in town knew much about Mr. Burns. He was a recluse. He seldom left his cabin in the woods except to come to town to buy food. He wanted to be as far away from people and civilization as possible.

The context of the passage tells you that a *recluse* is someone who wants to be alone and who shuns the company of other people.

Read the following passage and answer the question.

Example 1

There on the editorial page was a *caricature* of the mayor. The artist had made his nose bigger and his squinty eyes smaller, his belly fatter and his hands grasping—all to convey an impression of greed and corruption.

1   What is a *caricature*?

    A   a cartoon

    B   a painting

    C   an article

    D   an editorial

The correct answer is **A**, "a cartoon." The context clues in this passage describe how an "artist" had exaggerated the features of the mayor. Only A makes sense in this passage.

Here's another example:

Example 2

Railroad Power

Railroads began to crisscross their way across the whole country in the late 1800s. The people who were in charge of deciding where to lay the railroad track helped determine the success or failure of towns. The railroad's existence became *synonymous with* wealth. If your town was too far from the railroad, then it could mean that your town might not survive. Businesses and residents would leave producing ghost towns. But if your town was on the railroad line, businesses like restaurants, hotels, printing establishments, and stores would open to support the trade that the railroad brought. Owners of the first railroads wielded an uncanny power.

2   What is the meaning of the phrase *synonymous with* in the passage?

    A   outline

    B   equivalent to

    C   sounded like

    D   timely

The correct answer is **B**, "equivalent to." The passage goes on to say that if a railroad was absent, the town might die.

Strategies and Tips
for Using Context Clues

1. Look for context clues—either in the sentence in which an unfamiliar word appears, or in the sentences before or after it.

2. Use the substitution method. Substitute each answer choice for the underlined word in the passage. Choose the substitution that makes the most sense.

3. Sometimes a word is not defined by its context, but a closely related word is. For example, if the context tells you that *linguistic knowledge* is knowledge about language, you should be able to figure out what kind of scientist a *linguist* is when you see the word later in the selection.

3. When you answer vocabulary questions, be sure you are not fooled by a "false friend" word that looks like the vocabulary word, but is unrelated to It. For example, above, *Inherent* is not the same as *inherited*.

NOTICE: Photocopying any part of this book is forbidden by law.

49

Practice

Read the following paragraphs and answer the questions.

Selection 1

In 1907, the owner of the Barton Ranch in southwestern Hale County thought that a branch of the Santa Fe railroad line from Plainview to Lubbock was going to pass near or through his land. He drew up plans for a town to be called Bartonsite, which he believed would grow into a thriving town. So convinced was Joseph J. Barton that he built his Barton Home from an architectural plan book in a Victorian style. This elegant home was supposed to attract the railroad. By 1909, 250 people were living in Bartonville, eagerly awaiting the railroad's arrival. Unfortunately, the railroad ended up running several miles east of Bartonsite. Shortly thereafter, the commercial buildings from Bartonsite were *relocated* to Abernathy, thirteen miles to the southeast. By 1921, the Bartonsite post office closed, and Bartonsite became a ghost town. Only the Barton House still remains, carefully maintained.

1   What does the word *relocated* mean in this passage?

   A   taken apart

   B   moved to a different place

   C   offered for sale

   D   rebuilt

Selection 2

As Bartonsite failed, Abernathy, eighteen miles north of Lubbock, grew up around the railroad. With the buildings acquired from Bartonsite, Abernathy became a *prosperous* town. By 1910, it had its own post office. In the 1920s a flourmill and a cheese factory opened in the town. Within the next thirty years Abernathy acquired electricity, a sewer system, and a pubic water system. Then oil was discovered nearby, infusing new life into the town's businesses. Now the population of Abernathy is close to three thousand citizens consisting of about one thousand families.

2   What is the meaning of the word *prosperous* in this passage?

   A   dangerous

   B   railroad

   C   vanishing

   D   well-to-do

Section 3

Locations of towns throughout America still depend on economic stability, and often the *proximity* to transportation. After all, transportation means that businesses can exchange goods and materials, and people can travel to work. At first it was ships, then trains, automobiles, trucks, and airplanes. Since we can't get everything we need from our own communities, we have to reach out to other communities. That is why the railroads were once so important. That is also why Bartonsite failed to grow but Abernathy flourished.

3   What is the meaning of the word *proximity* in this passage?

   A   ability to get a train

   B   approximate

   C   how close you are to something

   D   if you can afford the train

Selection 4

Some people don't eat shellfish, like shrimp, lobster and crabs, because these animals are *scavengers*. They eat all the dead organic matter they can find on the bottom of the ocean floor; it is like riffling through the trash.

4   What does the word *scavengers* mean, and what information in the passage above gives you the clues for its meaning?

_____

_____

_____

_____

_____

_____

_____

8 Vocabulary 2: Clues from Word Parts

Knowing how words are put together can also help you to figure out the meanings of unfamiliar words. Look at the following sentence.

> Carlos tried to leap across the stream, but he *miscalculated* and fell in the water with a splash.

If you don't know the meaning of *miscalculate*, and the context does not help you, you can still figure it out if by taking the word apart.

- You probably recognize the base word, *calculate*. It means "to figure out."
- The prefix *mis-* means "wrong" or "badly." Now you know that Carlos figured out something wrong—either the distance or his jumping ability.

Here is a list of some common prefixes and suffixes. Read it over to familiarize yourself with them and their meanings.

COMMON PREFIXES AND SUFFIXES

Prefix	Meaning	Example
de-	from, down	**de**construct
dis-	away from, opposite	**dis**figure
il-, im-, ir-	not	**ir**regular
mis-	wrong, badly	**mis**use
pre-	before	**pre**soak
re-	again	**re**use

Suffix	Meaning and Part of Speech	Example
-able, -ible	worthy of, able to (adj.)	desir**able**
-ion, -tion	act of, state of (noun)	igni**tion**
-ize	cause to be, become (verb)	final**ize**
-ment	state of (noun)	punish**ment**
-or	one who (noun)	act**or**
-ous	full of, having (adj.)	fictit**ious**

Read the passage and answer the question.

Example 1

The pianist sat down at the piano ready to begin her concert, but she was very nervous and she felt disconnected. In order to *replenish* herself, she took a deep breath. Once she began to play she was fine. Breathing helped.

1   What is the meaning of *replenish* in the passage?

    A   disconnect

    B   make herself full again

    C   calm

    D   restart

B is the correct answer. The prefix *re-* gives you the clue you are looking for a word or phrase that includes "again." Even if you don't know the root word (it's Latin for "full"), you can guess at the meaning if you know the prefix *re-*.

Strategies and Tips
for Using Word Parts

1. To help you figure out the meanings of unfamiliar words, look for familiar prefixes and suffixes as well as for context clues.

2. The base part of a word is not always English. It may come from an ancient Latin or Greek word. But you may still be able to figure out some part of the meaning from the prefix or suffix alone. You might not know the meaning of the root *vert* in the word *revert*. (It comes from a Latin word meaning "turn.") But from the prefix *re-* you might be able to guess that it contains the idea of *again or back*. Of course, it means "turn back to" an earlier state or behavior.

Selections for Practice

Read the following selections and answer the questions.

Selection 1

Gary seemed friendly and encouraging. He even got Martin and Lucia to keep up with the group when they were lagging behind. But I still had a *premonition* that all was not right, that Gary was not what he seemed to be, that somehow we were being led into a trap.

1   What does the word *premonition* mean in this passage?

    A   a relaxed feeling of well-being

    B   a feeling that an unpleasant event is going to happen

    C   a widely accepted piece of information

    D   good advice

Selection 2

It was like listening to moms in stereo. My mother explained for the hundredth time why I couldn't have the car for the weekend, while my bossy older sister *interpolated* helpful remarks like "She's right, you know," "I tried to tell you," and "You just don't listen to Mom, do you?"

2   What are *interpolated* remarks?

    A   clever remarks

    B   remarks inserted between other remarks

    C   serious remarks,

    D   wise and thoughtful remarks

Selection 3

The town residents had worked for more than a year setting up a recycling system. Finally was a clear recycling plan in place. All the residents complied with the restrictions. People were feeling good about what they were doing, until they found out that the recyclables were getting put into the dump anyway. The residents' anger was *indescribable*.

3   What is the meaning of the word *indescribable* in the passage? How do you know that?

_____

_____

_____

_____

_____

9 Practice Selection

from Selma, Lord, Selma

by Sheyenne Webb

The following selection is by Sheyenne Webb, a young woman who joined Dr. Martin Luther King, Jr.'s freedom marches during the Civil Rights movement of the 1960s.

1   During those early days of the church meetings, before the first marches, I would be the only child there. I'd sit in back and listen. I hadn't told my mother and father about missing school.

2   We began practicing singing some of the freedom songs—*Ain't Gonna Let Nobody Turn Me 'Round, O Freedom, This Little Light of Mine*, and some of the others. I knew them all. So it was decided—and I don't remember exactly how—that I would be singing at some of the mass rallies to be held.

3   So I was now a part of the movement; the worry I had had about missing school vanished.

4   That evening when Rachel got home, we walked around the block several times, talking about the meetings. I told her about the songs.

5   "You gonna sing up there in front of everybody?" she asked. "Ain't you gonna be scared?"

6   "I don't know," I said. "I never been up there before a bunch of people."

7   There were more than eight hundred people at that first rally held at Brown Chapel the night of Sunday, January seventeenth, and some of the teachers were in that crowd. I didn't look at them.

8   Rachel and I—dressed in our best dresses and wearing ribbons—sat in the front row; I think we must have arrived an hour early. The Reverend Reese started the meeting with a short talk about the first march to be held the following day. After several minutes, he said it was time for a song and called for me.

9   I sang and the people all joined in. After a few stanzas of *Ain't Gonna Let Nobody Turn Me 'Round*, I noticed that Rachel was up there with me, beaming and singing her heart out. We would do a lot of singing together in the coming weeks.

10   Now, the singing at those meetings had a purpose; it wasn't just for entertainment. Those songs carried a message. They were different from Negro spirituals, which—as beautiful as they are—told of some distant hope while carrying the burdens of this life. Freedom songs cried out for Justice right now, not later.

11   The words were simple and clear. They spoke of our determination, our dignity:

12   `We shall not, we shall not be moved,
              We shall not, we shall not be moved,
          Just like a tree that's planted by the water,
              We shall not be moved.

13   And some told of the ultimate sacrifice we were prepared to make to achieve a dream:

14   O freedom, o freedom,
              O freedom's over me, over me,
          And before I'll be a slave
              I'll be buried in my grave,
          And go home to my Lord
              And be free.

15   Monday, January 18, was sunny and cool in Selma. There was a whole crowd of people waiting outside the church when I left the house. Dr. King was to arrive sometime that morning and the first march was to be held. As I waited, squinting up the street for a glimpse of him—or some reason I thought he'd come walking down Sylvan Street—I listened as some of the men talked about Sheriff Clark having a group of deputies waiting at the courthouse.

16   "Man, they got their clubs," said one of them. It made me more than a little nervous. I couldn't know—and surely didn't know—that the mayor of Selma, Joseph Smitherman, and the public safety director, Wilson Baker, had reached an "agreement" with the sheriff that there would be no undue force used. None of us could know that. So we waited with an air of uncertainty, but also with resolve and anticipation. Somebody started singing and the rest of us joined in; the singing bolstered our spirits.

17   Suddenly a woman shouted, "There he comes," and a long black car seemed to swish to the front of the church; there was a cheer as Dr. King alighted, smiling and waving. Because of my size, I couldn't get a good look at him. The crush of people straining forward wedged me to the fringes.

18   It wasn't long then that we began lining up on the sidewalk.

19   It occurred to me then that on this day, at any moment after the first step, somebody might die. We began moving forward, walking two or three abreast. It was about two blocks to Alabama Avenue and there Baker stopped us. I later learned that he told Dr. King that we didn't have a parade permit. So we broke up into small groups and walked piecemeal to the downtown.

20   Some of the people went into restaurants and stores with lunch counters and were served. I stayed with Mrs. Margaret Moore and we walked through the downtown for several minutes, then returned to the church. It wasn't until later that I learned that a white man attacked Dr. King as he registered at the Hotel Albert, located on Broad Street.

21   That night at the rally, me and Rachel sang again. There would be another march the next day, we were told. There was a tremendous cheer. Until then, I had been a little disappointed in the size of the crowd that had turned out for the march. But when I heard the shouting and the applause, I felt more confident.

22   I remember it was during one of those first rallies that I got up there by myself and sang a song that surely told what we had to face:

23   *I went down to the County jail,*
             Had no money to pay the bail,
          Keep your eyes on the prize,
                O Lord, O Lord.

Excerpts from Selma, Lord, Selma, by Frank Sikora. Copyright ©1979 by University of Alabama Press. Reprinted by permission of the publisher, University of Alabama Press

❖   ❖   ❖   ❖   ❖   ❖   ❖   ❖

Two months after these events, the Selma police brutally broke up a Civil Rights march, beating, gassing, and arresting several hundred people. Two marchers were killed. A horrified Congress passed a federal Voting Rights act, guaranteeing the marchers the rights they were demanding.

Use "from Selma, Lord, Selma" to answer questions 1-10

1 Why were the church meetings that Sheyenne Webb attended being held?

  A to ensure that everyone knew the same songs

  B to give the children practice in singing before an audience

  C to hold regular Sunday services

  D to prepare people for a civil rights rally

2 What words best describe Sheyenne Webb?

  A determined and courageous

  B light-hearted and funny

  C puzzled and uncertain

  D shy and retiring

3 Knowing the freedom songs made Sheyenne feel —

  A afraid that she would have to sing alone

  B safe and protected

  C part of the civil rights movement

  D proud of herself

4 The purpose of the songs was —

  A to carry the message that people wanted justice now

  B to demonstrate how well people sang

  C to entertain the listeners

  D to introduce people to the Negro Spiritual form

5 In paragraphs 13 and 14, what words help the reader understand what is meant by *the ultimate sacrifice?* —

  A freedom's over me

  B I'll be buried in my grave

  C to achieve a dream

  D we were prepared to make

6 Singing helped the marchers while they waited outside the church by —

  A bolstering the spirits of the demonstrators

  B calming the deputies

  C keeping the crowd together

  D preventing people from rioting

7 The songs Sheyenne sang expressed the people's —

  A anger and frustration

  B bitterness and fear

  C determination and dignity

  D weariness and hopelessness

8 In the line "Keep your eyes on the prize," (paragraph 22) what does "the prize" refer to?

  A freedom and the right to vote

  B meeting Dr. King

  C scholarship money for singing well

  D staying out of jail

9 Which of these is the best summary of this selection?

A Selma, Alabama, had an important place in the Civil Rights Movement. Sheyenne Webb sang there, and Dr. Martin Luther King led several freedom marches there. After several terrible events there, African Americans got the right to vote.

B Sheyenne Webb was a famous singer of the Civil Rights Movement. She sang for Dr. Martin Luther King, Jr., and she marched in Selma, Alabama. Her songs told of the distant hope the people had for freedom.

C Sheyenne Webb was a young schoolgirl in Selma, Alabama, at the time of the Civil Rights movement. She cut school to attend civil rights rallies with her friend Rachel. She learned the movement's songs of freedom, and sang them several times at rallies to inspire the people who attended.

D Sheyenne Webb's involvement in the Civil Rights movement in Selma, Alabama, began when she missed school to attend meetings and sing freedom songs that cried out for justice now. Her first freedom march, led by Dr. Martin Luther King, Jr., was stopped by Selma's public safety director. But at the rally that night she learned that there would be another march, and she sang her songs of freedom once more.

10 What was the mood of the crowd before the start of the march described in the selection? Support your answer with evidence from the selection.

_____

_____

_____

_____

_____

_____

_____

FEEDBACK AND COACHING TIPS

Now compare your answers with the correct ones. If you got an answer wrong, try to understand why.

1. Choice **D** is the best answer—the meetings were Civil Rights rallies. Singing was an important part of the meetings, but the meetings were not held primarily to have people learn the same songs (choice A). Although Sheyenne and Rachel got practice singing before an audience (choice B), this was not the purpose of the meetings, either. The meetings were held on school days, so they were not regular Sunday services (choice D).

> **Tip from the Coach**
>
> **When a question asks for the purpose of something, check to make sure that the answer you choose describes the main purpose, not less important or barely possible ones.**

> **Tip from the Coach**
>
> **When a question asks you to describe a person's character, choose three descriptions that can be supported by details in the selection, not one that is possible but unsupported.**

2. Choice **A** is correct: Sheyenne was both determined and courageous. She didn't let anything stop her from attending the rallies, and she marched in a march that could have ended in bloodshed—as a later march in Selma did. The other answer choices are either unlikely, given what we know of Sheyenne, or possible but not supported by the selection.

3. Paragraph 3 makes clear that choice **C** is the best answer. She may also have felt proud of herself (choice D), or afraid of singing alone at first (choice A), but the selection does not say this. Choice B is certainly wrong—Sheyenne knew she was doing something dangerous in joining the movement and singing its song.

> **Tip from the Coach**
>
> **The selection will probably make clear the nature of a character's feelings. Don't answer on the basis of feelings that you, rather than the character, might have.**

NOTICE: Photocopying any part of this book is forbidden by law.

61

Tip from the Coach

As always, your answers to questions like this one must receive support from the selection.

4. Choice **A** is the best answer, as paragraph 10 makes clear. They were not singing demonstrations or entertainment (choices B and C). And the paragraph specifically contrasts the purpose of the freedom songs with that of the older Spirituals, so choice D is also wrong.

5. Choice **B** is the best answer. The word ultimate means both "final" and "most important." Both meanings are conveyed by choice B: the ultimate sacrifice that the marchers faced was death. All the marchers knew that Civil rights workers and marchers had been killed. None of the other answer choices conveys this meaning.

Tip from the Coach

To understand the meaning of a word from its context, you frequently have to look at one or more sentences before or after the word in question.

6. Answer **A** is the correct one, as paragraph 16 makes clear. Nothing in the selection suggests that the singing affected the deputies (choice B), who were not even present, or that there was any danger of the people rioting (choice D). Choice C is improbable, since the crowd was not in danger of splitting up; that took place only after the march was stopped.

Tip from the Coach

Look at the selection carefully when you respond to a cause-and-effect question like this one, and don't be distracted by effects or events that either did not happen or that were not caused by what the question asks.

7. The answer is **C**. Refer to paragraph 11. All the other answer choices refer to negative emotions, which the people certainly experienced at one time or another—but the purpose of the songs was to banish emotions like these.

Tip from the Coach

Read the question carefully. Don't choose an answer that might be a true statement, but that does not answer the question that was asked.

62

8. Choice **A** is the best answer. This is the reason for the marches in Selma. The other answer choices are not the reason for the marches, and thus could not be the "prize" referred to in the song. A prize is usually something big—the wrong answer choices are not true prizes except, perhaps, for a particular individual in the case of choice C—and the song is not about a single individual.

> ### Tip from the Coach
>
> **When you look for the meaning of a metaphor like "the prize," think carefully about what the metaphor symbolizes. (More about metaphors in the next section of the book.)**

9. Choice **D** is correct. It covers the main events of the selection accurately and concisely. Choice A is not a good summary because the selection is not primarily about Selma—it is about Sheyenne Webb's participation in the events there. Choice B makes several factual mistakes: Sheyenne Webb was not a famous singer, and nothing in the selection says she sang for Dr. King. Choice C begins well, but it does not deal with the later events related in the selection.

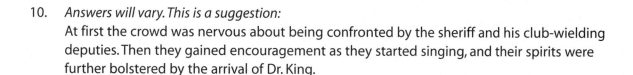

> ### Tip from the Coach
>
> **The correct answer to a summary question will apply to the entire selection, not to just a paragraph or two.**

10. *Answers will vary. This is a suggestion:*
    At first the crowd was nervous about being confronted by the sheriff and his club-wielding deputies. Then they gained encouragement as they started singing, and their spirits were further bolstered by the arrival of Dr. King.

UNIT 1
Reading

B. Analyzing Fiction

A work of fiction—a short story or a novel—uses many special devices to help tell the story. The more you know about these literary devices, the greater your understanding of the story will be—and the greater your pleasure in reading.

This chapter will review some of these devices for you. Start off by reading the story that begins on the next page. The chapter is based on it.

El Lobo Solo

1   The towering bronze figure of the Texas Ranger stood tall on its cracked concrete pedestal, looking down impassively at the yellow buses pulling up in front of the red brick building. Masses of students piled out, chattering and wiping sweat from their faces as they moved towards the wide steps. Small groups stopped to talk, unwilling to start what was bound to be a long, hot day. But the bell rang shrilly, and the last stragglers finally went in.

2   At least one Johnson High student wasn't in the building yet. A block away, Callie Gonzalez half walked, half ran along the sidewalk. She hoped that maybe, just maybe, the bell had not already rung. But even as she hoped, she knew she was late. *This will be my third late this month*, Callie thought. *And it's only the fourteenth!* She never wanted to be late—it just seemed to happen. With a huge sigh, she hurried along.

3   Being late upset Callie. It meant she was breaking the rules. "Rules are important, Callie," her mother always said. "Even when they don't seem to be important. Without rules, people cannot live together."

4   When it came to rules, Callie's mother was unbending. Mrs. Gonzalez was a lawyer who worked for the county—and a close family friend had been the famous *El Lobo Solo*—Captain Manuel "Lonewolf" Gonzaullas, a legendary Texas Ranger who single-handedly enforced the law in the oil fields of the 1920s. Callie had grown up hearing tales of Captain Gonzaullas, and she had adopted him as her hero, even though he had died before she was born. Maybe she and El Lobo Solo were even related, she thought—their last names were so similar. The statue of the Ranger in front of the school always reminded her of the Captain. She dashed past the statue, which looked down disapprovingly at her.

5   Being late was not the only thing Callie was worried about this morning, however. Last week, the Johnson High Student Council finished its charity drive. After weeks of bake sales, walkathons, and even a school fair, the council had collected over three hundred dollars. Today, the council would present the money to the director of a local charity. Callie was the council's treasurer—so the money was her responsibility. And it was a big responsibility! *Something bad could happen to that money*, she thought. *I won't be able to stop worrying until it's safe in the director's hands.*

6   When Callie got to school, she raced from the office to her homeroom class. She stared anxiously at the clock as the last few minutes ticked away. Finally, the bell rang, and she had a chance to go to the Student Council office and check on the money. Racing down the hall, Callie found the door to the office half open. Inside, papers were strewn all over the floor. The lockbox was on top of the desk. It had been pried open. The money was not there.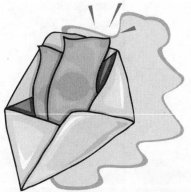

7   Wendy, the council president, and Lamar, the vice president, stood by the desk. "It's stolen. The money's stolen." Lamar

said, voicing what Callie could see for herself. "I called the principal," Wendy added. "He's on his way." She paused for a moment. "We made a promise to give that money to charity," she said. "I'm head of the student council, and I hate to say it, Callie, you were responsible for the money. If it's gone, you or your family may have to pay it back."

8   *But that's not fair*, Callie wanted to say. *It was stolen. It's not my fault*. But then came another thought. *What would El Lobo Solo do?* She took a deep breath. "You're right," she said. "I am the treasurer. This is my responsibility. And as treasurer, I am going to find that money—and bring it right back!"

9   Wendy and Lamar looked at Callie, mingled respect and anxiety in their eyes. Lamar spoke first: "If anyone can find the money, Callie, you can," he said. Callie smiled weakly. Wendy looked more doubtful. "Well, I hope you can find it fast," she said. "Mr. Archuleta from the charity is going to be here at three o'clock this afternoon. And right now . . ." Her eyes drifted to the clock ticking away on the wall. Nine fifteen. Callie gulped, realizing she had less than six hours to go.

10   Word that the money was gone—and that Callie had promised to find it—spread quickly through Johnson High School. As Callie prowled the halls, friends came over to say how sorry they were about what had happened. Whenever she ran into them, Lamar and Wendy offered their support.

11   But one student was not supportive at all. As Callie turned a corner, she found herself face to face with Jamie Conroy. He was a big, muscular senior with a nasty, surly attitude. Jamie smirked down at Callie, "I hear you're looking for some missing cash," he said. Callie nodded nervously. "What makes you think you're going to find it?" Jamie asked. "You could get hurt, you know."

12   He started to walk away, then turned back to glare at Callie. "Even a popular girl like you," he added menacingly.

13   Callie's eyes narrowed as she watched Jamie swaggering down the hall. *He knows something*, she thought. *What would El Lobo Solo do?* He'd follow him.

14   During each class, Callie fidgeted for the hour to be over. Between classes, the Lone Wolf tracked her prey. Somehow, the prey knew it—he kept looking back at her. But at least she knew exactly where he was every minute of that morning.

15   Then, at lunchtime, she lost him. *Where did he go?* she wondered. Feeling more and more foolish, she went out to the front of the school, looking all around like a squirrel trying to find a precious acorn that it had buried last year.

16   For several minutes she wandered around the schoolyard, stopping for a moment to seek comfort from the statue. Help me, Lobo Solo, she thought. The Ranger gazed back at her silently, one hand raised in command, his badge glinting in the sun.

17   Then Callie noticed something. There, on the far side of the statue, a figure was crouching. Jamie Conroy!

18   Callie hurried around the base of the statue. Someone was stuffing a bulging envelope into a crack in the statue's concrete base. Callie froze. The figure glanced up, yanked the envelope back from the crack, and stood up to face her.

19   It wasn't Jamie Conroy.

20   "I found the money," said Lamar. "It was here. The thief hid it in this crack."

21   Callie snatched the envelope out of his hand. "You found it? Liar! You took it! You're the thief," she shouted.

22   Lamar spread his hands and looked at her wide-eyed, innocent. "Hey, Callie, I didn't take it. I told you, I found it." Then his expression changed, and with no warning he leaped at her, grabbing for the envelope. Callie stumbled backwards, holding tightly to the envelope with both hands.

23   Suddenly, Callie saw a hand—a big hand. The hand grabbed the back of Lamar's neck, hard. Lamar shrieked and let go of the envelope. "Let's all go to see the principal," said Jamie Conroy, holding the struggling Lamar with one hand.

24   "Where did you come from?" was all Callie could say.

25   "You're welcome," said Jamie dryly. "I told you that you could get hurt. I've been keeping an eye on you all day—just in case."

26   "Thanks," said Callie weakly. She began to brush herself off, when she realized that she was still holding the envelope in her hand. She had caught the thief and recovered the money, all before three o'clock—just as she'd promised. Of course, she had a little help. But she could have done it by herself. She glanced at Jamie.

27   Somehow, just for a moment, he looked a little like her vision of El Lobo Solo.

NOTE: All the characters in this story are fictional, except for *"El Lobo Solo"*—Captain Manuel "Lonewolf" Gonzaullas. He was an actual Texas Ranger, one of the legendary figures of that organization. You can find out more about him at the Texas Ranger Hall of Fame and Museum in Waco (which he helped found), or at the Museum's web site.

1 Elements of the Writer's Craft

Setting

Simply put, **setting** is the time and place where the story happens. Usually, the author tells you the setting at the beginning of the story. Often, however, you can to figure it out for yourself from clues provided by the author.

Here is the first paragraph of the story you just read:

Example 1

1   The towering bronze figure of the Texas Ranger stood tall on its cracked concrete pedestal, looking down impassively at the yellow buses pulling up in front of the red brick building. Masses of students piled out, chattering and wiping sweat from their faces as they moved towards the wide steps. Small groups stopped to talk, unwilling to start what was bound to be a long, hot day. But the bell rang shrilly, and the last stragglers finally went in.

1a   Which of the following clues in the first sentence most clearly indicates that the story will take place in a school?

    A   There is a statue of a Texas Ranger.

    B   The statue's pedestal is cracked.

    C   There are yellow buses pulling up to the sidewalk.

    D   The building is made of brick.

The best choice is **C**. Yellow buses are school buses, so the setting is probably a school. Choices B and D do not tell us much—a statue of a Texas Ranger might be located in any public place in Texas, and the fact the statue's pedestal is cracked gives us no information whatsoever about the setting. By itself, choice D—the fact that the building is made of brick—does not strongly suggest that the setting is a school, since plenty of buildings are made of brick and plenty of schools are not.

1b   Which of the following clues in the second sentence suggests that the time of the story is in the morning?

    A   The school steps are wide.

    B   The students are chattering.

    C   The students are piling out of the buses.

    D   The students are wiping sweat from their faces.

The correct choice is **C**. Since the students are piling out of the buses and moving toward the school steps, the story probably begins at the start of the school day. The fact that they are chattering and sweating (choices B and D) tells us nothing about the time of day, nor does the fact that the school steps are wide (choice A).

Characters

Characters are the people who appear in a story. Just about every story ever written has characters—it would be hard to write a story without them! Characters draw readers into stories. Usually, a story focuses on one main character. This character is called the **protagonist**. Readers usually follow the action through the protagonist's eyes.

How can you be sure which character is the protagonist? Read the second paragraph of the story and then answer the question that follows it.

Example 2

2   At least one Johnson High student wasn't in the building yet. A few blocks away, Callie Gonzalez walked swiftly along the sidewalk. As she walked, she hoped that maybe, just maybe, the bell had not already rung. But even as she hoped, she knew she was late. *This will be my third late this month*, Callie thought. *And it's only the fourteenth!* She never wanted to be late—it just seemed to happen. With a huge sigh, she hurried along.

2   In paragraph 3, which of the following is the best indication that Callie will be the story's protagonist?

    A   Paragraph 3 includes italics.

    B   She is often late for school.

    C   The paragraphs show us Callie's thoughts.

    D   She walks to school instead of taking the bus.

Choice A pinpoints a typographical peculiarity of the third paragraph that has no real importance at all, so it is not the right answer. Choices B and D, on the other hand, both focus on differences between Callie and the other characters. Neither of these details, however, necessarily indicates that she is the protagonist. The correct choice is **C**. Callie's thoughts appear in paragraph 3, which is an almost sure sign she is the protagonist—we follow the story through her eyes and thoughts. (Other details also suggest this: she is the first character whose name we learn; she is the first character who appears as an individual in the story.)

 (Warning: This is a general rule, not a hard and fast one. For example, in the "Sherlock Holmes" detective stories, Holmes is the protagonist; his friend Dr. Watson, through whose eyes we witness the action, is merely the narrator, not the protagonist.**)**

Motivation

Of course, a story's characters don't just sit there. They do things—they meet each other, talk about the world around them, and sometimes even solve mysteries. In a well-written story, everything a character does is done for a reason. This reason is the character's **motivation**.

Character motivation is a very important part of fiction. To understand how motivation shapes stories, read the example below and answer the question that follows it.

Example 3

3   Being late upset Callie. It meant she was breaking the rules. "Rules are important, Callie," her mother always said. "Even when they don't seem to be important. Without rules, people cannot live together."

4   When it came to rules, Callie's mother was unbending. Mrs. Gonzalez was a lawyer who worked for the county—and a close family friend had been the famous *El Lobo Solo*—Captain Manuel "Lonewolf" Gonzaullas, a legendary Texas Ranger who single-handedly enforced the law in the oil fields of the 1920s. Callie had grown up hearing tales of Captain Gonzaullas, and she had adopted him as her hero, even though he had died before she was born. Maybe she and El Lobo Solo were even related, she thought—their last names were so similar. The statue of the Ranger in front of the school always reminded her of the Captain. She dashed past the statue, which looked down disapprovingly at her.

3   Based on paragraphs 3 and 4, Callie will be motivated to —

    A   find out if Captain Gonsuallas really looked like the statue

    B   lie and pretend she was not late

    C   live up to the rules and act on her own when necessary

    D   study hard in hopes of becoming a lawyer like her mom

The correct choice is **C**. In paragraphs 3 and 4, we learn how important rules are to Callie and how she admires "Lonewolf" Gonzaullas. Based on this information, we can predict that she will try to live up to the rules and act on her own when necessary. Choice B is unlikely, since we know that Callie has a strong respect for rules. Choice A is also unlikely. Since Captain Gonzaullas was a close friend of her family, she probably already knows what he looked like. Choice D uses information from paragraph 3, but nothing in the paragraph suggests that Callie wants to be a lawyer or even that the story is headed in that direction.

Foreshadowing

In **foreshadowing**, details in one part of a story give readers a hint about something important that is going to happen. If someone explains that he is afraid of heights, it may be a hint that the author will soon make him climb a high tower. Foreshadowing can make a story exciting by suggesting major events to come.

As you read the example below, think about what might lie ahead for Callie. Then use your reading to answer the question that follows.

Example 4

5 Being late was not the only thing Callie was worried about this morning, however. Last week, the Johnson High Student Council finished its charity drive. After weeks of bake sales, walkathons, and even a school fair, the council had collected over three hundred dollars. Today, the council would present the money to the director of a local charity. Callie was the council's treasurer—so the money was her responsibility. And it was a big responsibility! *Something bad could happen to that money*, she thought. *I won't be able to stop worrying until it's safe in the director's hands.*

4 As you know, the story is a mystery story. What statement in paragraph 6 foreshadows the problem that needs to be solved?

  A Something bad could happen to that money, she thought.

  B Callie was the council's treasurer.

  C Last week, the Johnson High Student Council finished its charity drive.

  D There were weeks of bake sales, walkathons, and even a school fair.

Choices B, C, and D do not seem to be foreshadowing anything—they seem to be straightforward statements without even a hint of an indication that something is going to happen. Choice **A**, however, focuses on Callie's worry—a worry that all too soon comes true. This is an example of foreshadowing.

Plot and Central Problem

The events in a story make up its **plot**. The plot is the action of the story, from the beginning to the end. Plots build—one event in a story seems to lead up to the next. The events that make up a well-crafted plot usually have a cause and effect relationship.

In this story, as in many stories, the plot is built around a **central problem**—a problem that the protagonist, or main character, must deal with in some way. Up to this point, however, the story has been concerned with the setting, introducing the main character, motivation, and the like. In the following paragraph, the plot begins to take off, as the central problem is introduced.

Example 5

6   When Callie got to school, she raced from the office to her homeroom class. She stared anxiously at the clock as the last few minutes ticked away. Finally, the bell rang, and she had a chance to go to the Student Council office and check on the money. Racing down the hall, Callie found the door to the office half open. Inside, papers were strewn all over the floor. The lockbox was on top of the desk. It had been pried open. The money was not there.

5   What is the central problem that Callie faces?

   A   checking on the money

   B   dealing with the principal

   C   getting to class on time

   D   recovering the money

The correct choice is **D**, "recovering the money." Choice A is not the central problem. Callie is able to check on the money—and she finds it missing. But how is she to do this? That's the central problem of the story. Choice B is vaguely possible, but it is not supported by the story. The principal does not even appear in the story, and dealing with him would not seem to be as great a problem as getting the money back. Choice C—getting to class on time—seems to be a problem that Callie has, but it is not what the story is about. It is not the central problem at all.

Conflict

One element in a story's plot is as important as cause and effect. **Conflict** drives almost every story's plot forward. Conflict is what makes a story interesting. The main character in a story—the protagonist—faces obstacles that block or complicate his or her efforts to deal with the story's central problem. Such obstacles may be people, circumstances, a puzzle, a deadline, or even a fear with which the protagonist must come to terms. The protagonist's struggle against these obstacles and complications forms the story's conflict.

Anything that the protagonist must overcome in order to accomplish his or her goal is part of the conflict. In Callie's case, the conflict involves all the obstacles to her recovering the money.

Reread the paragraph below and use your understanding of conflict to answer the question.

Example 6

7   Wendy, the council president, and Lamar, the vice president, stood by the desk. "It's stolen. The money's stolen." Lamar said, voicing what Callie could see for herself. "I called the principal," Wendy added. "He's on his way." She paused for a moment. "We made a promise to give that money to charity," she said. "I'm head of the student council, and I hate to say it, Callie, you were responsible for the money. If it's gone, you or your family may have to pay it back."

8   *But that's not fair,* Callie wanted to say. *It was stolen. It's not my fault.* But then came another thought. What would El Lobo Solo do? She took a deep breath. "You're right," she said. "I am the treasurer. This is my responsibility. And as treasurer, *I am* going to find that money—*and bring it right back!*"

9   Wendy and Lamar looked at Callie, mingled respect and anxiety in their eyes. Lamar spoke first: "If anyone can find the money, Callie, you can," he said. Callie smiled weakly. Wendy looked more doubtful. "Well, I hope you can find it fast," she said. "Mr. Archuleta from the charity is going to be here at three o'clock this afternoon. And right now . . ." Her eyes drifted to the clock ticking away on the wall. Nine fifteen. Callie gulped, realizing she had less than six hours to go.

6   Which of the following is not part of the conflict?

A   Callie or her family may have to pay back the money if it is not recovered.

B   Mr. Archuleta is coming for the money at three o'clock.

C   No one knows who the thief is.

D   Wendy and Lamar were the ones who discovered the theft.

All four choices deal with the theft and its consequences. However, choice **D** is the only one that is not part of the conflict. The fact that Wendy and Lamar discovered the theft doesn't constitute an obstacle or complication to recovering the money. All the other choices are involved in the conflict. Choice A describes a consequence if the money is not recovered in time; choice B sets a deadline; choice C is the major obstacle to the recovery of the money. All the other items are obstacles or complications. Choice B set's a deadline.

The Antagonist

Conflicts can be about more than time or circumstances or other impersonal forces. Often, protagonists come into conflict with other characters. A character that provides such conflict is called the **antagonist**.

Example 7

10   Word that the money was gone—and that Callie had promised to find it—spread quickly through Johnson High School. As Callie prowled the halls, friends came over to say how sorry they were about what had happened. Whenever she ran into them, Lamar and Wendy offered their support.

11   But one student was not supportive at all. As Callie turned a corner, she found herself face to face with Jamie Conroy. He was a big, muscular senior with a nasty, surly attitude. Jamie smirked down at Callie, "I hear you're looking for some missing cash," he said. Callie nodded nervously. "What makes you think you're going to find it?" Jamie asked. "You could get hurt, you know."

12   He started to walk away, then turned back to glare at Callie. "Even a popular girl like you," he added menacingly.

13   Callie's eyes narrowed as she watched Jamie swaggering down the hall. *He knows something*, she thought. *What would El Lobo Solo do? He'd follow him.*

7   At this point in the story, the main antagonist appears to be—

A   El Lobo Solo

B   Jamie Conroy

C   Lamar

D   Wendy

Choice **B** is correct. As the possible thief, Jamie is an antagonist—a character who stands between Callie and her goal of recovering the money. Choice A is clearly wrong: El Lobo Solo is Callie's inspiration, not her antagonist. And at this point in the story, neither Lamar nor Wendy (choices C and D) appear to be obstacles to getting the money back.

NOTICE: Photocopying any part of this book is forbidden by law.

75

Figurative Language: Similes and Metaphors

In literature, words can sometimes mean more than just what a dictionary says they mean. When authors use words to mean something extra, beyond their literal meaning, they are using **figurative language**. Figurative language can enrich the meaning of any story.

A common form of figurative language compares things that seem to have nothing in common except one important thing that the writer chooses to emphasize. An author might write that an athletic woman is *like a cat*. This comparison emphasizes the woman's surprising agility and alertness.

- When such a comparison uses the words *like* or *as*, it is called a **simile**.

- An implied comparison that does *not* use *like* or *as* is called a **metaphor**. Like similes, metaphors show readers the unusual qualities of the people, places, or things in a story. Because they do not call attention to themselves, however, they are subtler than similes.

The example below uses both these kinds of figurative language to make comparisons. Read the examples and then answer the questions that follow.

Example 8

14   During each class, Callie fidgeted for the hour to be over. Between classes, the Lone Wolf tracked her prey. Somehow the prey knew it—he kept looking back at her. But at least she knew exactly where he was every minute of that morning.

15   Then, at lunchtime, she lost him. *Where did he go?* she wondered. Feeling more and more foolish, she went out to the front of the school, looking all around like a squirrel trying to find a precious acorn that it had buried last year.

8a In sentence 2 of paragraph 14, the metaphor calls Callie "the Lone Wolf." What characteristic of a wolf does the author wish to emphasize?

    A It howls at the moon.

    B It is a cunning and silent hunter.

    C It is a fierce and powerful fighter.

    D It is at home in cold weather.

Choice **B** is the best answer—Callie is tracking Jamie, like a cunning and silent hunter. Choice A is clearly irrelevant—Callie is not howling or doing anything like howling. Choice C is a true statement about wolves, but it is not the reason for the metaphor, since Callie is stalking Jamie, not fighting him. Choice D is clearly irrelevant, since we know from paragraph 1 of the story that the weather is hot, not cold.

Now look at paragraph 15, which contains a simile.

8b In the last sentence of paragraph 15, the simile describes Callie as "looking all around like a squirrel trying to find a precious acorn that it had buried last year."

    A She is anxious and uncertain

    B She is keen-eyed and alert

    C She is relaxed and confident

    D She is tense and angry

Think of a squirrel, trying to puzzle out exactly where it buried a nut some seasons ago. It sits on its hind legs, stretches upward, looks around, flicks its tail, makes a short run, and repeats the performance. It is clearly anxious and uncertain, as Choice **A** suggests. The other choices are not appropriate to Callie's behavior, especially since in the first part of the sentence she is described as feeling "more and more foolish."

Symbolism

Symbolism is an important literary element. One detail in a story—an object, a place, a person's name, and so on—can be used to represent something else. Authors often use symbols to add levels of meaning to their stories. A warm and cozy house, for example, might *symbolize* the happiness of the family that lives inside.

As you read the following passage, keep your eyes open for a symbol. What meaning does the symbol add to the story?

Example 9

16   For several minutes she wandered around the schoolyard, stopping for a moment to seek comfort from the statue. *Help me, Lobo Solo*, she thought. The Ranger gazed back at her silently, one hand raised in command, his badge glinting in the sun.

9   In paragraph 13, the statue of the Texas Ranger symbolizes—

    A   a secret place where Jamie Conroy can hide the money.

    B   Callie's frustration at losing track of Jamie Conroy.

    C   the protection by rules that makes Callie and other students feel secure.

    D   the edge of the schoolyard.

Choices A and D both describe literal meanings of the statue. It does mark the edge of the schoolyard, and it does seem to be a place for Jamie Conroy to hide the money. But the question asks what the statue *symbolizes*—in other words, what else it represents. Choice B is not the statue's literal meaning, but paragraph 13 shows that the statue eases Callie's feelings of frustration. The correct choice is **C**. The statue of a lawman represents the rule and makes Callie—and her classmates—feel secure.

Plot Twist

A good story does not always proceed in a straight line from the statement of the central problem to its conclusion. It would be boring if it readers could always figure out ahead of time everything that was going to happen in the story. So authors often throw in unexpected happenings designed to surprise the reader. These author surprises are often referred to as **plot twists**. The story you have been reading has a plot twist near the end—sometimes called a **surprise ending**.

Read the next part of the story, and notice the plot twist.

Example 10

17   Then Callie noticed something. There, on the far side of the statue, a figure was crouching. Jamie Conroy!

18   Callie hurried around the base of the statue. Someone was stuffing a bulging envelope into a crack in the statue's concrete base. Callie froze. The figure glanced up, yanked the envelope back from the crack, and stood up to face her.

19   It wasn't Jamie Conroy.

20   "I found the money," said Lamar. "It was here. The thief hid it in this crack."

21   Callie snatched the envelope out of his hand. "You found it? Liar! You took it! You're the thief," she shouted.

22   Lamar spread his hands and looked at her wide-eyed, innocent. "Hey, Callie, I didn't take it. I told you, I found it." Then his expression changed, and with no warning he leaped at her, grabbing for the envelope. Callie stumbled backwards, holding tightly to the envelope with both hands.

10   What is the plot twist in the story?

    A   Callie sees a figure crouching behind the statue.

    B   Callie snatches the envelope from Lamar's hands.

    C   Lamar claims to be innocent.

    D   The real antagonist turns out to be Lamar, not Jamie.

The answer is clearly choice **D**. It turns out that Lamar is the thief, not Jamie. This is an unexpected turn of events, and qualifies as a plot twist. The other choices are all occurrences in the story, but none is an unexpected turn of events. None is a plot twist.

Resolution

Of course, few stories end with their main characters—their protagonists—in the middle of tense conflicts, unable to achieve their goals. The conflict has to be worked out, or resolved. The point in a story when the conflict ends and the protagonist achieves his or her goals is called the **resolution**. The resolution is an important element that ties together the plot. Without it, most readers would not be satisfied with the story's ending.

Read this final example, paying attention to how the story's conflict is resolved. Then answer the question that follows.

Example 11

23   Suddenly, Callie saw a hand—a big hand. The hand grabbed the back of Lamar's neck, hard. Lamar shrieked and let go of the envelope. "Let's all go to see the principal," said Jamie Conroy, holding the struggling Lamar with one hand.

24   "Where did you come from?" was all Callie could say.

25   "You're welcome," said Jamie dryly. "I told you that you could get hurt. I've been keeping an eye on you all day—just in case."

26   "Thanks," said Callie weakly. She began to brush herself off, when she realized that she was still holding the envelope in her hand. She had caught the thief and recovered the money, all before three o'clock—just as she'd promised. Of course, she had a little help. But she could have done it by herself. She glanced at Jamie.

27   Somehow, just for a moment, he looked a little like her vision of El Lobo Solo.

11   What event in the story is most important in bringing about its resolution?

    A   Callie asks Jamie where he came from.

    B   Callie sees something of El Lobo Solo in Jamie.

    C   Jamie grabs Lamar by the neck.

    D   Jamie says that he has been keeping an eye on Callie all day.

The correct choice is **C**. Once Lamar is captured, there are no more obstacles to the return of the money. The central problem is resolved. Choices A and B are details in the story, but neither is an event that ends the conflicts and resolves the central problem. Choice D is important to the plot, but the resolution does not come when Jamie decides to keeps an eye on Callie. It comes when Jamie captures Lamar after Callie discovers Lamar was the thief.

Strategies and Tips
for Understanding Elements of the Writer's Craft

The TAKS test will ask you to analyze pieces of fiction. As you've seen, this means you will need to answer questions about literary elements. To answer such questions successfully, you need to keep these elements in mind as you read. Here is a handy list of strategies to help you focus on the elements of the writer's craft.

1. **Setting.** Where and when does this story take place? What details—especially at the beginning of the story—reveal this information? How does the setting affect the story's characters and plot?

2. **Characters.** Which character is the story's central focus—its protagonist? How can you tell that he or she is the main character?

3. **Motivation.** What reasons do the characters have for behaving the way they do? What details in the story reveal those reasons?

4. **Foreshadowing.** Does the author give you hints about events that may happen later in the story? What details suggest or foreshadow future events?

5. **Plot and Central Problem.** What is the relationship between the events in the story? How does the plot build?

6. **Conflict.** What obstacles does the main character have to overcome in order to accomplish his or her goals? Are the obstacles such forces as time? How does the author use these obstacles to create conflict? How does the conflict drive the story forward?

7. **Antagonist.** Are the obstacles other characters, or antagonists?

8. **Figurative Language.** Does the author use language with figurative, non-literal meaning? Does the story include metaphors or similes, comparisons between things that are not really similar? How does the figurative language enrich the story's meaning?

9. **Symbolism.** Are there any details in the story that represent something other than themselves? What do these details symbolize? How do they affect the story's meaning?

10. **Plot Twists.** Are there one or more plot twists, in which the plot takes an unexpected turn? Is there a surprise ending—a plot twist at the very end of the story that leads to an unexpected resolution?

11. **Resolution.** How does the main character overcome the obstacles he or she faces and achieve his or her goals at the end of the story? How does the author resolve the story's conflict and tie together its plot? Is the resolution satisfying?

Practice

Read the following excerpt from a longer story, and answer the questions.

Fire!

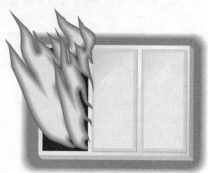

1   After he paid for his purchase, Gus moved slowly towards the door of the store. He was still getting used to having a cast on his leg. Walking with crutches was difficult and tiring; he could only move slowly. Awkwardly clamping his paper bag between his teeth, he managed to open the door and step outside.

2   It was a Saturday morning in early autumn. The sky was streaked with just a few clouds, and the sun shone clearly. A dry breeze blew down the street. The weather was beautiful; this was always Gus's favorite time of year. Right now, though, not even the beauty of the day could bring his spirits up. It was the height of the football season, his team needed him— and here he was with a broken leg, barely able to move. *I can't believe I was dumb enough to turn down Mom's offer of a ride*, he thought.

3   With a sigh, he began to struggle down the sidewalk. As he pulled himself along, the breeze began to pick up, turning into a gusting wind. The scream of a distant fire siren tore the air. It came closer, and Gus saw to his horror that the fire trucks were turning down the short dead-end street leading to his house.

4   With worry creasing his forehead, Gus gripped his crutches and tried to move faster. But he found he couldn't. Every effort made his shoulders and arms smart. Still, he pushed forward. The smell of smoke assailed his nostrils. One block went by, then two. By the time he turned into his street, he could see a column of black smoke like a giant snake in the air. It was coming from his house.

5   No longer feeling any pain, Gus raced down the street on his crutches. Smoke was pouring from the kitchen window. Firemen and fire hoses seemed everywhere, but there didn't appear to be any real damage. Outside the house stood his mother, looking terrified, and his younger brother Darryl, looking embarrassed. "What happened?" was all Gus could say.

6   "It was an accident," his mother answered. Darryl hung his head low and looked the other way. "Your brother was just cooking his breakfast and the grease caught on fire, and then the paper

towels caught on fire. He did the right thing and put the towels in the sink, but then the curtains caught on fire—" Gus could feel the ache in his limbs now as he looked from his brother to the kitchen window and back again. "It wasn't your brother's fault," his mother added, "it was an accident."

Darryl was always doing things like this, and Mom was always making excuses for him…

1   In paragraph 1, the most important thing we learn about Gus is that —

   A   he has a broken leg and is on crutches

   B   he has just bought something at the store

   C   he leaves the store

   D   he needs to hold the bag in his teeth to open the door

2   How does the setting of this story contrast with Gus's mood?

   A   Gus is pleased because it is his favorite type of day.

   B   It is a beautiful day, but Gus is in a glum mood.

   C   The weather is unpleasant, but Gus is happy.

   D   The wind is dry, but it is the height of the football season.

3   What is the most important problem Gus faces in this selection?

   A   He must overcome his broken leg and crutches to race several blocks.

   B   He cannot decide what to buy at the store.

   C   He is in a bad mood because he cannot enjoy the weather.

   D   His brother has put him in a difficult situation.

4   Gus tries to move faster in paragraph 4 because—

   A   he is concerned about his house

   B   he is in a hurry to get home and rest

   C   he wants the several blocks he has to walk to go by faster

   D   he wants to get better at walking on crutches

5 What details best convey Gus's concern and anxiety as he hurries home?

   A his blaming himself for not accepting his mom's offer of a ride

   B his desire to help his football team

   C the creases in his forehead, his grip on the crutches, and the pain in his shoulders

   D the difficulty he has carrying the bag from the store

6 How does the simile in paragraph 4 contribute to the mood of the selection?

   A It indicates how painful it is for Gus to run on crutches.

   B It shows readers that the smoke is in a long column that stretches upward.

   C It suggests that the smoke is threatening and dangerous.

   D There is no simile in paragraph 4.

7 In paragraph 5, why is Gus finally able to move without pain?

   A He is healing more rapidly than he realized.

   B His concern for his house and family cause him to forget the pain

   C His pain was just imaginary

   D The exercise has helped drive the pain away.

8 At the end of the selection, Gus is probably —

   A amused by the entire situation

   B annoyed with his mother for not driving him to the store

   C embarrassed that the fire trucks came to his house for no reason

   D relieved that the house is safe and disgusted with his brother

2 Theme

Why do we read fiction? Certainly, it is enjoyable—but we don't read fiction just to be entertained. Good fiction offers readers valuable insights about life. The insight a work of fiction offers readers—the message its author tries to communicate—is called its **theme**.

Every serious piece of fiction can be said to have a theme. Sometimes, authors want to make absolutely sure readers understand their messages. In such a work, an author might make his or her theme *explicit* by stating it directly:

> This is the story of the most important day of my life—the day I learned that all people are responsible for their own actions—even me.

More often, though, the theme isn't stated out loud like that. Usually, it is *implied*. To understand the theme, readers have to pay close attention to the elements of fiction. Through plot, character, setting, symbolism, and the other elements of the writer's craft, the author will give readers a special insight on life.

The TAKS test may require you to answer questions about theme. To answer them, you have to read fiction carefully and analyze its the elements. Because this involves so much careful thought, questions about theme will often be *open-ended*. (But not always—questions about main idea and summary questions often contain elements of theme.)

Open-ended questions do not include answer choices. But this is not the only difference. An open-ended question is often less specific than a multiple-choice question. Instead of asking you about a particular image, paragraph, or plot event, it may ask you to explain what you have learned from a story or what insight the story offers. And open-ended questions will almost always require you to include examples from the story that support your ideas. You will need to write several sentences in response.

To learn about theme and answering open-ended questions, we'll look closely at a piece of fiction. After reading, we'll look at two responses to an open-ended question on its theme—a successful response and an unsuccessful response. We'll analyze what makes one more effective than the other. Then, you'll have a chance to improve the less successful response.

Example 1

The New Girl

1   Gillian arrived late for her first day at Killeen High. As she entered the building, a bell rang to signal the end of a class period. The halls quickly filled with students. They gathered around lockers or charged from room to room. Everyone seemed to be talking and laughing in little groups. No one even looked at Gillian. The only greeting she got was a hurried "Excuse me" when someone bumped into her.

2   Gillian sighed and slowly walked to the office. She always hated the first day at a new school. It always came in the middle of the year. All the students were already locked into their own little social worlds, leaving her—the "new girl"—out in the cold. And it happened so, so often! Gillian was proud of her father. He was an officer in the U.S. Army who led an exciting life. She loved to hear stories about his experiences. Having him for a father made her happier than anything else in the world.

3   But Gillian hated having to move again and again. Each time, she had to start over. At first, she tried to meet people at each new school. But it was hard to do. None of the little groups wanted to welcome her in. Sometimes people were even mean to her, making fun of her whenever she tried to fit in. It seemed as if she would get hurt every time she let her guard down. So Gillian stopped trying. She had her pride, which gave her some solace when she felt lonely. But it was getting to the point where she was growing up without friends.

4   By the time her father transferred to Fort Hood, though, she was at least used to it. *I'm sure I'll be miserable here*, she thought, *but I know the routine, anyway*. She found the office, where an emotionless man gave her a schedule and told her to report to Mr. Guadalupe's Social Studies class. Once she was there, Mr. Guadalupe had her stand up in the front of the room and introduced her to the class. Gillian didn't think she could stand it. *How embarrassing*, she thought.

5   The students in the room smiled politely at Gillian as she stood before them. Then she sat at an empty desk near the back of the room. As she expected, every student in the room turned his or her attention away from her. *I might just as well not be here*, she thought, *for all they care*.

6   It was always like this, every time. Gillian figured she was looking forward to months of lonely, lonely school days. She sighed as she turned her full attention to the teacher, who was beginning to lecture. Then she noticed a smiling face nearby. A girl sitting two desks away was smiling at her. Gillian started to smile back, but hesitated. *That girl's probably just waiting for a chance to be mean to me*, she thought. So she looked away. But she couldn't help glancing over again. The girl was still smiling.

7   The day seemed to drag on forever. Each classroom was the same as the last one—and Gillian was ignored in each. Finally, the last bell rang. *At last!* Gillian thought. *Now I can go home*. No more sitting in silence, worrying that the people around her were waiting for a chance to hurt her feelings. She just had to stop at her locker, and then she'd go straight home.

8   But a funny thing happened. Standing at the locker next to Gillian's was the girl from Mr. Guadalupe's class. She smiled at Gillian again. This time, Gillian managed a quick, tight smile—but a smile all the same.

9   "Hi," the girl said, extending her hand. "I'm Francesca."

10   It was the first time all day another student had spoken to Gillian. She wasn't quite sure how to respond. Her eyes searched Francesca's face, but all they found was that smile. Her smile was friendly, open, and sincere. Slowly, Gillian took her hand and shook it. "I'm Gillian," she said.

11   "I know," said Francesca. "Mr. Guadalupe introduced you to the class." Of course, Gillian thought. *How stupid of me. Now comes the teasing*. Only Francesca didn't tease. "Isn't it awful being the new girl?" she asked. "I transferred here in the middle of last year. It was tough."

12   Gillian gazed at Francesca with amazement. Here was someone who had been through it too—who knew how she felt! "It *is* awful," she said. "My dad's in the military, and we move a lot. I really hate it."

13   Francesca smiled. "I'm sorry," she said sympathetically. "But you'll make it. I mean, I did. My dad used to be in the military, too."

14   Gillian smiled shyly. "Thanks," she said. "I'll see you tomorrow." She started to walk away.

15   "Wait!" Francesca called out. Gillian turned. "Which way are you headed?" she asked. "Maybe we can walk home together."

16   It turned out they lived near each other. Gillian left the building with Francesca, talking about their families and their

experiences as the "new girl." Maybe, Gillian thought as they walked, *just maybe, this time things really will be OK.*

1   What lesson about life does Gillian learn in this story? Support your answer with evidence from the story.

_____

_____

_____

_____

Analyzing a Successful Response to an Open-Ended Question

The open-ended question above requires readers to explain what Gillian—the *protagonist* or main character of this story—learns about life. Readers learn this lesson with her. In other words, it asks about the story's *theme*, the insight about life it communicates.

A response to this question must be a complete paragraph. It should, first of all, state what Gillian learns about life (and thus state the story's theme). But a successful response will do more than just this. A successful response will explain the theme instead of just stating it. Furthermore, a successful response will support its ideas with examples or *evidence* from the story, just as the question asks. Finally, a successful response will tie the explanation and evidence together with a *conclusion*.

Oscar read "The New Girl" carefully and wrote a successful response to the open-ended question. Your response might not be exactly the same as his, but his response contains all the elements that make a response successful.

Let's analyze it to understand what makes it so successful. Read Oscar's response below, then answer the questions that follow it.

Oscar's Response

In this story, Gillian learns that you have to open yourself up to people if you want your life to be happy. She worries that new people will hurt her, but she decides to take a chance and trust Francesca. When Gillian started at other schools, people were mean to her. But Francesca is kind and sincere. Because Gillian learns to trust her, she will be much happier at her new school.

1   Oscar's response starts with a simple answer to the question—a statement of what Gillian learns about life. This is the **main point** of Oscar's response.

   On the lines below, write Oscar's main point.

   _____

   _____

2   After he presents his main point, Oscar **explains** the lesson that Gillian learns in more detail. This explanation offers more insight into the story's theme.

   On the lines below, write the explanation of Oscar's main point.

   _____

   _____

3   Next, Oscar offers **evidence** to support his main point. He includes two specific examples from the story that back up his ideas.

   On the lines below, write Oscar's first example.

   _____

   _____

   Now write Oscar's second example on the lines below.

   _____

   _____

4   Finally, Oscar ties his point, explanation, and examples together with a **conclusion**. Based on what he has already written, he offers one final thought about the lesson that Gillian learns in the story.

   On the lines below, write Oscar's conclusion.

   _____

   _____

   _____

   _____

   _____

   _____

Revising an Unsuccessful Response to an Open-Ended Question

As you've discovered, Oscar's response to the open-ended question on "The New Girl" is successful because it does several things. First, it offers a simple answer to the question—in this case, stating the story's theme. This answer is Oscar's main point. Second, it explains the main point in greater detail, developing Oscar's idea further. Third, it supports the main point with evidence—two examples from the story. Fourth, it ties everything together with a conclusion—a final thought on the story's theme.

But not every response is as successful as Oscar's. When an answer to an open-ended question is missing one or more of these elements, it is not successful. This is not a reason to give up, however. An unsuccessful response can be a starting place. With careful **revision**, even an unsuccessful response can be as successful as Oscar's.

Below is another open-ended question about the theme of "*The New Girl.*"

2   Why is Gillian unhappy at the beginning of this story? How does she change? Support your answer with details from the story.

A successful response to this open-ended question would be a complete paragraph. It would make a clear main point, explain that point, support it with evidence from the story, and end by drawing a conclusion. But Carl's answer, which appears below, does not meet these requirements.

Carl's Response

Gillian is unhappy because she doesn't have any friends until she meets Francesca.

What keeps Carl's response from being successful? First of all, it's only one sentence long—not a complete paragraph. Carl offers a simple answer to the question. This could serve as a main point. But he doesn't explain or support his ideas. And he does not include a conclusion.

Even so, this can be the starting point for a very successful response to the open-ended question. Help Carl revise his answer by answering the questions below.

1   Carl starts with a very simple answer to the question—he states why Gillian is unhappy and suggests how she changes. But to be an effective main point, this sentence needs to be clearer about how Gillian changes.

Revise the sentence on the lines below.

_____

_____

2   Now Carl needs to explain his main point in more detail. By saying more about how Gillian changes, he can develop his ideas further.

Write a new sentence explaining Carl's main point on the lines below.

_____

_____

3   Next, Carl needs to support his ideas with evidence—details from the story that back up his main point. Help Carl choose his first example from the story.

Write a new sentence with a supporting example on the lines below.

_____

_____

4   Another piece of evidence would help make Carl's response even more successful. Pick a second example for him.

Write a new sentence with a second supporting example on the lines below.

_____

_____

5   Finally, Carl needs a conclusion to finish his response. His final thought should tie the whole paragraph together.

Write a new concluding sentence on the lines below.

_____

_____

NOTICE: Photocopying any part of this book is forbidden by law.

91

Strategies and Tips
for Responding to Open-Ended Questions

A successful response to an open-ended question consists of several sentences that…

1   state a main point…

A good main point offers a basic answer to the question. If the question deals with theme, the main point should state the author's message.

2   explain the main point…

Develop the main point further by explaining it in greater detail. For open-ended questions dealing with theme, you can explain the insight into life that the story communicates.

3   support the main point with evidence…

A successful response includes evidence from the story that supports the main point. When you are writing about theme, the best evidence is an example from the story that illustrates the author's message clearly.

4   and tie it all together with a conclusion.

Finally, draw a conclusion from the response you've written. For responses to open-ended questions about theme, your conclusion can be a final thought about the insight into life that the story communicates. Perhaps you can connect the story's theme to your own life?

Responding to an Open-Ended Question on Your Own

Now try to construct your own successful response to an open-ended question. First, read the story below. An open-ended question about the story's theme follows it.

Example 2

Disappointment

1   Junius sat on the bench for a long time. Everyone else had already gone home, but he still sat there. It was hot, but his football uniform was damp with sweat, making him shiver in the slight breeze. Still, he sat on the bench, not moving a muscle. He felt like crying, but he was just too tired.

2   He was too tired—and too disappointed.

3   All summer, Junius had practiced out in the back yard with his dad. Junius's dad had played football when he was in high school, and he still had a good arm. He was teaching Junius to be a wide receiver. He would throw the ball, and Junius would run after it. He got good—he could catch every pass. Junius knew he was fast enough. He showed it over and over, all summer long. His dad was proud. "You'll make the team, for sure," he said, over and over again.

4   Junius *was* good—out in the yard. But that afternoon at the tryouts, it was a different story. Suddenly, it wasn't just him and his dad. There were other players—bigger players. They threw the ball higher than Junius could reach. Sometimes other players, taller players, could put their hands just over him and slap the ball away. "Sorry, son," the coach said to Junius. "You're fast, but you're just not tall enough. Maybe when you grow a little more, you'll make the team."

5   Junius had been crushed. The coach saw it, and told him, "Good try. See you next year, OK?" But it didn't matter. He slumped onto the bench and sat there. He watched the other boys finish tryouts, watched the lucky few get picked for the team, and watched everyone pack up and leave. And he still sat there.

6   Finally, Junius got up and started for home. With every step, he thought about his dad. He could see his dad's smiling face, bursting with pride each time Junius ran so fast and caught the ball. "You'll be the best receiver the team ever had," he had said. The memory of the words made Junius's stomach hurt. He was upset he hadn't made the team—truly, he was deeply, deeply disappointed. But it was his dad's disappointment that he was really upset about.

7   Junius and his dad had had their ups and downs over the years. Sometimes they were really close to each other, and Junius's dad would call him his "best buddy." Other times, there would be distance. When work was tough and stressful, Junius's dad would be in another world. And if Junius's grades slipped—they didn't often, just once in a while—the distance would be there again. Junius's dad never seemed to get mad. He just pulled back. And that hurt Junius more than anything.

8   But that summer, that whole summer, they had been close—closer than they'd ever been. Junius's dad loved football, and loved playing it with him. When Junius did well, his dad was so happy—and that made Junius happy. He wanted to be on the team for himself. But even more so, he wanted to be on the team to make his dad happy. That way, they could stay that close.

9   Now, Junius was sure his dad would be disappointed. And when he got disappointed, he pulled away, off into some private world where Junius wasn't invited.

10   As Junius neared his house, he realized he'd waited so long that his dad was already home from work. *I'm coming home so late*, Junius thought, *he must be thinking that I made the team*. He could feel tears building in his throat. He didn't want to come home sobbing. But he couldn't keep a few tears from slipping out of his eyes and rolling down his cheeks.

11   Junius went around the house, to the back yard. Sure enough, there was his dad—football in hand. When he heard Junius approaching, he turned around fast, a big smile on his face.

94

12   Then something funny happened. Junius's dad stopped, paused for just a second or two. He saw Junius's face. His smile flickered, then resolved itself. He put down the ball, walked over to Junius, and gave him a big, big hug. "It's OK, son," he said.

13   Now Junius's tears came. His dad held him tight until they slowed and stopped. Then he stepped back and patted Junius on the shoulder.

14   "We've got a little time before dinner, buddy," he said, still smiling at Junius. "You want to play a little catch?"

15   Junius grinned. "OK, Dad."

Responding to an Open-Ended Question on Your Own

Here is another example of a question that asks you to construct your own response:

Why is Junius worried after tryouts? What does his dad teach him when he gets home? Support your answer with details from the selection.

To construct a successful response to this open-ended question, it is important to use the strategies you've already learned. Answering the following questions will help you get started.

1   First, think of a **main point** that answers the question simply, stating why Junius is worried and what his dad teaches him.

   Write your main point on the lines below.

   _____

   _____

2   Next, **explain** your main point, developing the idea in a bit more detail.

   Write your explanation on the lines below.

   _____

   _____

NOTICE: Photocopying any part of this book is forbidden by law.

95

3   Now you need **evidence** from the story that will support your main point. Choose a detail from the story that will give you some of the evidence your response needs.

Write your first detail on the lines below.

_____

_____

4   One more piece of **evidence** will make your response more effective. Choose a second detail from the story to support your main point.

Write your second detail on the lines below.

_____

_____

5   Finally, your response needs a **conclusion**. Can you come up with one last thought that will tie your whole response—main point, explanation, and evidence—together?

Write your conclusion on the lines below.

_____

_____

You can now put together a complete, one-paragraph response to the open-ended question, based on your answers to the questions above. If you've answered them carefully, your response should be as successful as Oscar's. Remember to write in complete sentences, and to use your own words when you write about details from the story.

Write your final response on the lines below.

_____

_____

_____

_____

_____

_____

3 Practice Selection

Below is an excerpt from the novel *The Bluest Eye* by Toni Morrison. Read it and answer the questions that follow.

from **The Bluest Eye**

by Toni Morrison

1   We walked down tree-lined streets of soft gray houses leaning like tired ladies. . . . The streets changed; houses looked more sturdy, their paint was newer, porch posts straighter, yards deeper. Then came brick houses set well back from the street, fronted by yards edged in shrubbery clipped into smooth cones and balls of velvet green.

2   The lakefront houses were the loveliest. Garden furniture, ornaments, windows like shiny eyeglasses, and no sign of life. The backyards of these houses fell away in green slopes down to a strip of sand, and then the blue Lake Erie, lapping all the way to Canada. The orange-patched sky of the steel-mill section never reached this part of town. This sky was always blue.

3   We reached Lake Shore Park, a city park laid out with rosebuds, fountains, bowling greens, picnic tables. It was empty now, but sweetly expectant of clean, white, well-behaved children and parents who would play there above the lake in summer before half-running, half-stumbling down the slope to the welcoming water. Black people were not allowed in the park, and so it filled our dreams.

4   Right before the entrance to the park was the large white house with the wheelbarrow full of flowers. Short crocus blades sheathed the purple-and-white hearts that so wished to be first they endured the chill and rain of early spring. The walkway was flagged in calculated disorder, hiding the cunning symmetry. Only fear of discovery and the knowledge that we did not belong kept us from loitering. We circled the proud house and went to the back.

5   There on the tiny railed stoop sat Pecola in a light red sweater and blue cotton dress. A little wagon was parked near her. She seemed glad to see us.

6   "Hi."

7   "Hi."

8   "What you all doing here?" She was smiling, and since it was a rare thing to see on her, I was surprised at the pleasure it gave me.

9   "We're looking for you."

10   "Who told you I was here?"

11   "The Maginot Line."

12   "Who is that?"

13   "That big fat lady. She lives over you."

14   "Oh, you mean Miss Marie. Her name is Miss Marie."

15   "Well, everybody calls her Miss Maginot Line. Ain't you scared?"

16   "Scared of what?"

17   "The Maginot Line."

18   Pecola looked genuinely puzzled. "What for?"

19   "Your mama let you go in her house? And eat out of her plates?"

20   "She don't know I go. Miss Marie is nice. They all nice."

21   "Oh, yeah," I said, "she tried to kill us."

22   "Who? Miss Marie? She don't bother nobody."

23   "Then how come your mama don't let you go in her house if she so nice?"

24   "I don't know. She say she's bad, but they ain't bad. They give me stuff all the time."

25   "What stuff?"

26   "Oh, lots of stuff, pretty dresses, and shoes. I got more shoes than I ever wear. And jewelry and candy and money. They take me to the movies, and once we went to the carnival. China gone take me to Cleveland to see the square, and Poland gone take me to Chicago to see the Loop. We going everywhere together."

27   "You lying. You don't have no pretty dresses."

28   "I do, too."

29   "Oh, come on, Pecola, what you telling us all that junk for?" Frieda asked.

30   "It ain't junk." Pecola stood up ready to defend her words, when the door opened.

31   Mrs. Breedlove stuck her head out the door and said, "What's going on out here? Pecola, who are these children?"

32   "That's Frieda and Claudia, Mrs. Breedlove."

33 "Whose girls are you?" She came all the way out on the stoop. She looked nicer than I had ever seen her, in her white uniform and her hair in a small pompadour.

34 "Mrs. MacTeer's girls, ma'am."

35 "Oh, yes. Live over on Twenty-first Street?"

36 "Yes, ma'am."

37 "What are you doing 'way over here?"

38 "Just walking. We came to see Pecola."

39 "Well, you better get on back. You can walk with Pecola. Come on in while I get the wash."

40 We stepped into the kitchen, a large spacious room. Mrs. Breedlove's skin glowed like taffeta in the reflection of white porcelain, white woodwork, polished cabinets, and brilliant copperware. Odors of meat, vegetables, and something freshly baked mixed with a scent of Fels Naphtha.

41 "I'm gonna get the wash. You all stand stock still right there and don't mess up nothing." She disappeared behind a white swinging door, and we could hear the uneven flap of her footsteps as she descended into the basement.

42 Another door opened, and in walked a little girl, smaller and younger than all of us. She wore a pink sunback dress and pink fluffy bedroom slippers with two bunny ears pointed up from the tips. Her hair was corn yellow and bound in a thick ribbon. When she saw us, fear danced across her face for a second. She looked anxiously around the kitchen.

43 "Where's Polly?" she asked.

44 The familiar violence rose in me. Her calling Mrs. Breedlove Polly, when even Pecola called her mother Mrs. Breedlove, seemed reason enough to scratch her.

45 "She's downstairs," I said.

46 "Polly!" she called.

47 "Look," Frieda whispered, "look at that." On the counter near the stove in a silvery pan was a deep-dish berry cobbler. The purple juice bursting here and there through crust. We moved closer.

48 "It's still hot," Frieda said.

49 Pecola stretched her hand to touch the pan, lightly, to see if it was hot.

50   "Polly, come here," the little girl called again.

51   It may have been nervousness, awkwardness, but the pan tilted under Pecola's fingers and fell to the floor, splattering blackish blueberries everywhere. Most of the juice splashed on Pecola's legs, and the burn must have been painful, for she cried out and began hopping about just as Mrs. Breedlove entered with a tightly packed laundry bag. In one gallop she was on Pecola, and with the back of her hand knocked her to the floor. Pecola slid in the pie juice, one leg folding under her. Mrs. Breedlove yanked her up by the arm, slapped her again, and in a voice thin with anger, abused Pecola directly and Frieda and me by implication.

52   "Crazy fool . . . my floor, mess . . . look what you . . . work . . . get on out . . . now that . . . crazy . . . my floor, my floor . . . my floor." Her words were hotter and darker than the smoking berries, and we backed away in dread.

53   The little girl in pink started to cry. Mrs. Breedlove turned to her. "Hush, baby, hush. Come here. Oh, Lord, look at your dress. Don't cry no more. Polly will change it." She went to the sink and turned tap water on a fresh towel. Over her shoulder she spit out words to us like rotten pieces of apple. "Pick up that wash and get on out of here, so I can get this mess cleaned up."

54   Pecola picked up the laundry bag, heavy with wet clothes, and we stepped hurriedly out the door. As Pecola put the laundry bag in the wagon, we could hear Mrs. Breedlove hushing and soothing the tears of the little pink-and-yellow girl.

55   "Who were they, Polly."

56   "Don't worry none, baby."

57   "You gonna make another pie?"

58   "'Course I will."

59   "Who were they, Polly?"

60   "Hush. Don't worry none," she whispered, and the honey in her words complemented the sundown spilling on the lake.

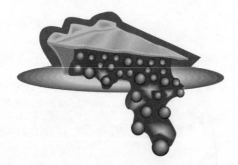

1 This story is told in the form of a —

  A biographical sketch

  B first-person narrative

  C magazine article

  D third-person narrative

2 Who is Mrs. Breedlove's daughter?

  A Claudia

  B Frieda

  C Pecola

  D The little girl with yellow hair

3 How does the description of the setting in the opening paragraphs prepare the reader for what happens in this selection?

  A It shows the reader that part of the town is polluted by the steel mills.

  B It shows the reader that the town is divided into two very different neighborhoods.

  C It shows the reader that the town is filled with beautiful houses and yards.

  D It shows the reader that the town is on one of the Great Lakes, bordering Canada.

4 What conclusion can you draw about the narrator, her sister, and their friend Pecola?

  A They are African-American, living in a segregated town.

  B They are tired of small-town life and want to get out.

  C They dream of owning beautiful lakefront houses.

  D They want to play with the little yellow-haired girl

5 What detail helps tell you that Mrs. Breedlove is a maid, not the owner of the big white house?

  A her glowing skin

  B her white uniform

  C the cooking odors

  D the polished cabinets

6 What makes Claudia, the narrator, so angry with the little girl with yellow hair?

  A her lack of respect for Mrs. Breedlove

  B her rudeness to Claudia and Frieda

  C the silly slippers she's wearing

  D her carelessness with the berry cobbler

7 What makes Mrs. Breedlove get angry?

  A Frieda and Claudia taste the berry cobbler.

  B Pecola knocks the berry cobbler onto the floor.

  C Pecola teases the little girl with yellow hair.

  D The little girl with yellow hair is not as respectful to her as her own daughter.

8 Why does the narrator say "her words were hotter and darker than the smoking berries" when Mrs. Breedlove yells at Pecola, Claudia, and Frieda?

  A to show how difficult it was to understand Mrs. Breedlove

  B to show how frightening Mrs. Breedlove had become

  C to show how loud Mrs. Breedlove's voice was

  D to show how much Mrs. Breedlove cared about the berry cobbler

9 Which sentence best states the main idea of this selection?

  A Claudia sees and hates the inequality between the races.

  B Pecola is awkward and unable to do anything right.

  C The girls are all fascinated by the woman called "The Maginot Line."

  D Claudia, Frieda, and Pecola try to make friends with a little girl with yellow hair.

10 In this selection from *The Bluest Eye*, how does the author contrast Mrs. Breedlove's treatment of Pecola and her treatment of the little girl with yellow hair? Support your answer with evidence from the story.

_____

_____

_____

_____

_____

_____

_____

_____

FEEDBACK & TIPS FROM THE COACH

Now compare your answers with the correct ones. If you got an answer wrong, try to understand why.

1. The correct answer is Choice **B**, because it is a story told by the person who experienced these events. It uses first-person pronouns—we (We walked down tree-lined streets of soft gray houses …) I, and me (…I was surprised at the pleasure it gave me). Choice D is partially correct because the selection is a narrative—it tells a story. However, it is not told in the third person (that is, by an outside observer using pronouns like he, she, and they). Choices B and C are also incorrect, because this narrative selection does not have the features of either an article or a biographical sketch.

Tip from the Coach

When you read a story, be sure you know what the point of view is. If the narrator uses I or we, you know that the story is told in the first person. If the narrator uses he, she, or they, you know that the story is told in the third person.

Tip from the Coach

In a narrative with several characters, it's important to keep track of the names of the characters and their relationships with the other characters. If you get these wrong, you won't understand the story correctly.

2. Pecola is Mrs. Breedlove's daughter—Choice **C**. You might have been confused because Pecola calls her mother "Mrs. Breedlove," and "ma'am," not "Mom" or "Mother." But paragraph 44 makes it clear that Pecola is Mrs. Breedlove's daughter. The little girl with yellow hair (choice D) lives in the house where Mrs. Breedlove works, but is not her daughter. Paragraph 34 tells us that Claudia, the narrator, and Frieda (choices A and B) are Mrs. MacTeer's girls, not Mrs. Breedlove's.

3. All of these are true or partially true statements about the setting. However, the question asks about the connection between the setting and the plot—that is, what happens in the story. Choice **B** is the correct answer, because the events in the story and the narrator's reaction to them are related to the fact that the town is divided into two separate neighborhoods. Choice C is only partially true because there are beautiful houses in only one part of town. The part of town in the story is not polluted by steel mills (choice A), and the fact that the town is on the shores of Lake Erie (choice D) is not important to the plot of the story.

Tip from the Coach

If there are many details of the setting, the author probably put them in for a reason. Ask yourself what's important about the setting, and pay attention to the way the setting is connected to the rest of the story. You probably won't find the answer stated directly in the story; you will need to figure it out by reading the whole story.

4. The best answer is Choice **A**. Choice B may be tempting because there are some details that indicate at least one of the girls wants to travel to bigger cities, but this is not true of them all. Choice C is incorrect because, although the girls admire the lakefront houses, the author never says that they dream of owning one. Only Choice A makes a true statement about all three girls. Notice, however, that these facts are only implied in the story. You need to infer them from details like African American people were not allowed in the park, and so it filled their dreams. Finally, the girls show no desire to play with the little yellow-haired girl (choice D).

Tip from the Coach

Pay careful attention to the details the author provides about the characters, and try to avoid jumping to conclusions. You may need to read quite a bit of the story before you can be sure which details best describe the characters.

Tip from the Coach

Questions like this one ask you to read between the lines—to infer something that is not stated directly. As you read the descriptive details in a story, you need to ask yourself, "Why is the author telling me this? What does it reveal about the characters?"

5. Although the details given in all the answer choices are accurate details from the part of the story that describes Mrs. Breedlove, only one is relevant to the fact that Mrs. Breedlove is a maid—her white uniform (Choice **B**). Notice that the author never states that Mrs. Breedlove is a maid. You have to infer it from her appearance, her actions, and her words.

6. Again, each answer has some elements that make the choice look correct. However, you can rule out Choice D because it is Pecola, not the little girl with yellow hair, who knocks over the berry cobbler. Choices A and C might look good because the little girl with yellow hair is wearing silly slippers and is not very friendly to Claudia and Frieda. But the narrator's anger really erupts when she hears the little girl call Mrs. Breedlove "Polly." Therefore Choice **A** is the correct answer.

Tip from the Coach

When you are asked a question about the characters' actions, read the details of the story carefully. Only some of the details will give you clues about what causes a character to behave in a particular way.

Tip from the Coach

Watch out for cause-effect questions. Look for the details that link one character's words or actions to another's.

7. You might pick Choice D as the correct answer because it states something that happens in the story. However, the little girl's lack of respect is not what Mrs. Breedlove is reacting to when she gets angry. Choice **B** is correct because this is the action that directly triggers Mrs. Breedlove's anger. Choices A and C are incorrect because they do not state things that happen in the story.

8. All the answer choices might seem possible at first. Mrs. Breedlove's voice may have been loud (choice C), she may have been difficult to understand (choice A), and she was certainly upset about the berry cobbler (choice D). But Choice **B** is the best answer because it most accurately shows how angry Mrs. Breedlove was at her daughter's carelessness and the mess that had been made on the clean kitchen floor.

Tip from the Coach

When you are asked a question about the author's language, you need to think carefully about what images the choice of words suggests—and what kind of emotional response the reader might have to these words.

9. The best answer is choice **A** because it makes a generalization that draws together Claudia's observations about the town at the beginning of the selection and the main event of the story (in the kitchen with Mrs. Breedlove). Choice B is a statement about one part of the selection, but not about the selection as a whole. Choice C is a minor detail, and choice D does not happen in the story at all.

Tip from the Coach

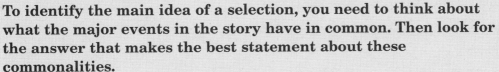

To identify the main idea of a selection, you need to think about what the major events in the story have in common. Then look for the answer that makes the best statement about these commonalities.

10. *Possible Answer:* The author shows that Mrs. Breedlove seems to be stricter with her own daughter than with the little girl with yellow hair. The little girl can call her "Polly," but Pecola has to call her "Mrs. Breedlove." She also seems to care more about the little girl than she does about Pecola. When Pecola gets hurt by the hot juice from the berry cobbler, Mrs. Breedlove hits her and yells at her. The little girl doesn't get hurt, just frightened, but Mrs. Breedlove hugs her and promises to make her another pie.

UNIT 1
Reading

C. Visual Literacy

Literacy includes more than just reading words alone. We are all surrounded by visual material that we "read"—ads, charts and tables, comic strips, Web sites, photos, drawings, and so on. The TAKS test will test you on your ability to understand the important points made in visuals like these—what it calls **"viewing and representing pieces."**

In the actual test, the viewing and representing piece will be part of the triplet—the group of three selections that share a common theme. The questions associated with the viewing and representing piece will probably test you to see if you understand how this common theme is treated in the visual. This short chapter will give you some practice with the kinds of questions that deal with the theme and purpose of a visual and with the points that it is making.

Example 1

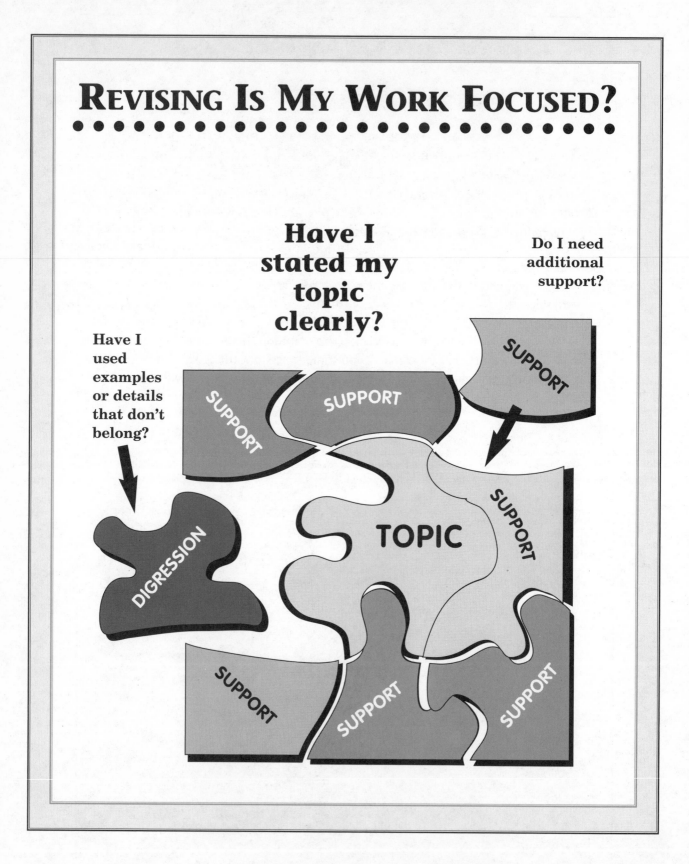

1a   The purpose of the visual in the writing poster on the facing page is to show that —

    A   a topic and its support have different shapes

    B   a topic and its support can be represented as dark and light gray shapes

    C   a topic and its support fit together like the pieces of a jigsaw puzzle

    D   a written composition can be represented as a square

Choice **C** is best. A composition is represented as a jigsaw puzzle, with a central topic and support items that fit into it. It is a visual representation of a simile that says, *A composition is like a jigsaw puzzle, with the topic and its support fitting neatly together like puzzle pieces.* The color of the pieces (choice B) and the fact that the completed composition will be a square (choice D) are arbitrary, and don't convey a message about the process of composition. The fact that a topic and its support have different shapes (choice A) is not important by itself. What is important is that they fit together to make a whole.

1b   What visual method is used to show that a digression doesn't belong in the composition?

    A   The digression piece is shown as a dark gray.

    B   The digression piece is shown outside the main body of the puzzle.

    C   The digression piece is the wrong shape to fit in the puzzle.

    D   The word **digression** is slanted.

The jigsaw puzzle pieces all fit together—except for **digression**, which is the wrong shape (choice **C**). All the other choices apply to at least one of the support pieces as well as to the **digression** piece, and so cannot show anything unique about the digression.

Practice

Selection 1

The cartoon below features Joey, an emotionally challenged snake from outer space, and his monkey friend Durwood.

2a What graphic device does the cartoonist use to show that Joey the snake comes from someplace other than Earth?

A Joey has big eyes.

B Joey has rattles at the end of his tail.

C Joey is wearing a space helmet.

D Joey's eyebrows are above his head.

2b The main message of this cartoon is that —

A being a friend sometimes means having to say you're sorry

B it's useless and self-destructive to worry about things that can't be changed

C monkeys are not always afraid of snakes

D the snake is a visitor from another planet

Selection 2

TIRED OF YOUR POKY OLD HOME COMPUTER?

Pick up a NEW *MANGO*® computer with faster processor, flat panel display, PLUS one year America Onboard® Internet access!

MANGO 300K

- Strontium® 6 Processor 1.8GHz
- 128MB DDR SDRAM
- 40 GB Hard Drive
- 15" LCD Flat Panel Display (15" viewable)
- 56K modem

PLUS!

One year free
America Onboard® Internet access!

Price: $949
Shipping and handling extra

MANGO 300K Plus

- Strontium® 6 Processor 2.0GHz
- 256MB DDR SDRAM
- 80 GB Hard Drive
- 17" LCD Flat Panel Display (17" viewable)
- 56K modem

PLUS!

One year free
America Onboard® Internet access!

Price: $1329
Shipping and handling extra

Mango PCs use genuine Macrohard® Doorway® Operating Systems
http://www.mango.com/home/dealoftheweek.shtml

Selection 2

2a What is the purpose of the two columns of information in this ad?

A They allow the viewer to compare two models of the Mango computer.

B They are there to fool the viewer into thinking that the Mango is a good computer.

C They give technical information for the use of computer professionals only.

D They try to persuade the viewer that the Mango is superior to other computers.

2b The ad tries to catch a viewer's eye by —

A appealing to his or her sense of humor

B giving useful technical information

C playing on his or her fear of appearing hopelessly out of date

D warning that old computers sometimes fail

2c The last line of the ad is —

A additional technical information about the computer

B the computer model reference code

C the Internet site of the manufacturer

D the manufacturer's FAX address

Selection 3

Languages of the World

Total Number of World's Languages
6060

Total World Population
6.2 Billion

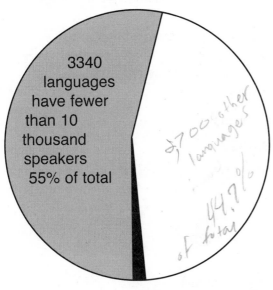

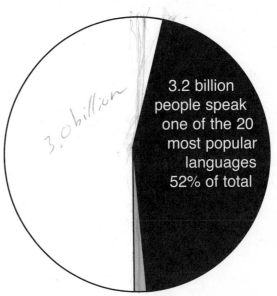

▲ 20 most popular
languages
0.3% of total

▲ fewer than 18.6
million people speak
one of the 3,340
rarest languages
0.3% of total

KEY

Languages with the most speakers

Languages with the fewest speakers

Other Languages

3a What do these two diagrams compare?

    A the 20 most popular languages and the 20 least popular

    B the number 6060 and the number 6.2 billion

    C the number and age of the world's languages

    D the number of the world's languages and the number of their speakers

3c According to the diagrams —

    A 0.3% of the world's people speak 0.3% of the languages

    B 18.6 million people speak the 20 most popular languages

    C most people in the world speak 52% of the languages

    D over half the world's people speak one of only 20 languages

3d The diagrams also show that —

    A 0.3% of the world's people speak the 20 most popular languages

    B 2700 people speak 44.5% of the languages

    C English is the language spoken by the most people in the world

    D only 18.6 million speakers account for over half the world's languages

3d From the diagrams, how many languages seem in the greatest danger of disappearing within the next 100 years?

    A 3340

    B 2700

    C 20

    D none

UNIT 2
Writing

In the writing portion of the TAKS test, you will be given a particular topic and asked to write a composition on that topic. You are free to choose the approach that in your mind best suits the topic. In other words, your composition could describe a personal experience, define a term, discuss your point of view, or your own experience. (Poetry is not accepted.) The lessons in this unit will guide you through several successful approaches and techniques, but other approaches are possible.

On the actual test, the prompt for your essay will be based on a theme common to the triplet— the two reading selections and the visual literacy selection that you will have already worked with on the test. Thus, in reading the selections and answering the multiple-choice questions, you will already have explored some aspects of the topic of the prompt. When you write your essay, you may wish to analyze or refer to a part or parts of the triplet in the composition, but you do not have to.

In the chapter that follows, you will work with a prompt similar to the one on the actual TAKS test. In each of the two Practice Tests at the end of the book, you will work with a prompt that is thematically linked to the triplets of the test.

Preparation for Writing a TAKS Composition

Teen TV Productions

Teen Values Production Company is coming to your town SOON! And we're LOOKING FOR MODELS! But we're not talking about people who can try on clothes or makeup—we're talking about the people who really count in your town. We're looking for ROLE MODELS!

Here's the catch! We don't know the good people in your town—and YOU DO! We need your help in finding them. Please write us on one of the topic listed below. Whichever topic you choose, be sure to let us know what the term "role model" means to you.

- Who do you know in your hometown who serves as a role model for high school students? What does that person do or say that makes him or her a good role model?

- Tell us why it is important to have good role models while you are growing up. Use examples from your own life and experience.

- What kinds of role models are best for you to have in growing up? Can a sports figure or an astronaut serve as a role model? Or should a role model be someone close to home that you can talk to?

If we like your ideas, you can be a production assistant for the show and we'll credit you at the end of the episode.

WRITE US RIGHT NOW! PLEASE!

The ad could have asked you simply to name a good role model. But then the producers would have to interview everyone that was named. By asking you to explain what you mean by role model and tell about your own experiences, they'll be able to choose the people they want to interview.

The 10th Grade TAKS English Language Arts test also asks you to write a composition based on ideas you found in the special reading section. You can also use your own life and experiences. This unit will get you ready to write that kind of composition.

1 What Makes a Good Composition?

Eduardo's class has been discussing what kind of role models it is important for students to have while they are in school. After the discussion, he wrote a draft of a composition about picking good role models. Here is what he wrote.

1   *When I was in middle school, we had an assembly every year about choosing good role models. One year Captain Michaels, the local fire chief, told us that when he was a kid, his next-door neighbor was a firefighter. Captain Michaels remembered hearing his neighbor whistling and singing every time he came home from his shift. He looked tired, but happy. That's when Chief Michaels decided to become a firefighter. Another time, Doctor Maria Santiago said she became a doctor because she liked the way her family doctor always talked to her.*

2   *By the time I left middle school, I thought that a role model was someone who helped you pick a career. Last year I discovered that there were role models all around me—students right here in school. These role models didn't show me what career path to take. They helped me live my life better right now, while I'm still in school. These role models showed me how to keep my eyes open in my daily life and how to step up when someone needed help.*

3   *For example, when I was a freshman, some tough kids started giving me a hard time right after last period. A senior saw what was happening and stepped in to help. He didn't have to do that, but he did it anyway. After I thanked him, I asked him why he helped. He looked surprised and said, "Because you needed help." So I learned that doing the right thing doesn't take a lot of thought. You see what's going on and you try to make things better.*

4   *Another time, I broke a bone in my leg and had to stay in the hospital for a week. It was the review week before finals, and I knew I was going to miss out on tips that would help me in the exams. A girl I barely knew who was good in math called me and said she'd like to help me review. I jumped (well, I didn't jump of course) at the chance, and she worked with me every day after school. I never felt so prepared in my life. At the end I asked her*

if there was some way I could repay her. She said, "Just pass it on. Help someone else."

5   Finally, just a few weeks ago, something very strange happened. My girl friend Selena told me that I was a role model for her younger brother. It seems that when he and his girl friend split up, Ysele told him that if he had treated her the way I treat Selena, she would not have broken up. Of course, I was flattered, but I really didn't know what Ysele meant. Selena gave me a look, but then she said, "Ysele likes the way you treat me. You ask me something and you listen. You tell me when I look OK and you help me do the things I want to do—like trying out for the basketball team." I never knew that I could be a role model, but I'm happy to be one. It doesn't take very much—all you have to do is to treat people the way you want to be treated yourself.

6   When I started high school, I thought that good role models were people outside my everyday life. Now I know that a good role model can be someone you see every day. They are people who seem to do the right thing easily, without thinking about it. They are good helpers as well as good friends. They can even tell you why a particular behavior is important, and they make you want to act the same way. So take a good look at the people in your everyday life and choose someone to show you the way.

Eduardo's composition is an example of a successful piece of writing because:

- Each paragraph has **focus**, and the composition as a whole shows **coherence** by connecting all the ideas.

- The composition shows **organization** by moving logically from idea to idea.

- The writing is thoughtful and insightful and exhibits effective **development of ideas** through examples and anecdotes.

- The composition shows the author's **voice** from the opening sentence to the end by expressing an individual point of view.

Journal Entry: Making Connections

What do you think? What did you like about Eduardo's composition?

_____

_____

Do you have a similar experience you can write about?

_____

_____

Let's analyze each part of Eduardo's composition to see how he constructed his response.

A. The Opening: Paragraphs 1 & 2

Eduardo catches the reader's attention by using anecdotes that do not form part of his final definition. Taking a chance like this is called "compositional risk" and gets the writer a Score Point of 4 in Development of Ideas. How does he do this?

The composition begins with two anecdotes in the first paragraph.

What idea do the anecdotes support?

_____

_____

What do you think the second paragraph will focus on?

_____

_____

NOTICE: Photocopying any part of this book is forbidden by law.

119

In paragraph 2, Eduardo does something different, although his general topic remains the same.

In the opening sentence of this paragraph, Eduardo sums up what he thought a role model was. Write his opinion below.

_____

_____

The rest of paragraph 2 shows how he has redefined the concept "role model."

In your own words, write Eduardo's definition of a role model.

_____

_____

What effect does Eduardo's technique have on the reader?

_____

_____

_____

_____

_____

Compositional Risk and Focus

When you finish reading the first paragraph, you know that Eduardo will be focusing on the concept of role model. At the end of the first paragraph, you think that you know what aspect of role model he will continue to develop. But you will be wrong.

At the beginning of the second paragraph, he tells you that because of the presentations at assembly he thought that a **"role model was someone who helped you pick a career."** Then, in the very next sentence he adds a new idea: **"I discovered that there were role models all around me—student right here in school."** Eduardo has kept the focus on the concept of "role model," but he has taken the reader on a journey from one interpretation to another. Writers call this pattern, "I USED TO THINK XYZ, BUT NOW I THINK QXR." Such a pattern is effective, because it keeps the reader involved. But there is a risk—the writer must know ahead of time how he or she really means to define a concept. Only the reader should be surprised.

B. The Body: Paragraphs 3-5

Organization

In paragraph 2, Eduardo introduces the idea that he has learned a lot from the role models he finds in school. This statement gives him the organization he needs for the rest of the composition.

How does the plural form of the word "role models" provide Eduardo with a guide to organizing his paper?

_____

_____

The reader now expects that the body of the composition will consist of examples and anecdotes demonstrating the kinds of role models he has encountered. If Eduardo organizes his composition well, each paragraph will consist of a separate anecdote.

Development of Ideas

When Eduardo chose to organize his composition by using three different anecdotes, he had to make sure that each paragraph followed the same structure. Here is the pattern he used:

Transitional Word — Anecdote — What the role model taught him.

What did Eduardo learn from the senior in paragraph 3?

_____

_____

What did Eduardo learn from the girl who tutored him in paragraph 4?

_____

_____

What did Eduardo learn from his girl friend and his own behavior in paragraph 5?

_____

_____

Voice

In writing, **voice** is what makes your composition individual. What you write about, what you choose to explain or define comes from your own thoughts and experiences. A composition that is written in your own voice does not sound like a formula. As a matter of fact it couldn't sound like a formula because you are different from everyone else who writes on this topic. The examples you choose are unique to you. The significance of an experience is something personal to you.

One way to establish voice is to make sure that the examples you choose come from your own life, experience, and observations. To show you how voice works, use the structure that Eduardo used in his body paragraphs to tell an anecdote about role models. Use your own experience, and don't forget to end with a line or two about what you learned.

_____

_____

_____

_____

_____

_____

_____

_____

(By the way, you've just written one of the paragraphs in what will be your own essay.)

C. The Closing: Paragraph 6

Completeness

A good closing gives a composition a sense of completeness. Does Eduardo have an effective closing paragraph?

> **Write one sentence from the closing that you particularly like.**

_____

_____

Notice that Eduardo makes use of ideas he has been exploring all along, but he does not repeat anything word for word. For example, the first line of the closing paragraph refers to paragraph 1 and the opening of paragraph 2.

> **Write another line from the closing and tell what paragraph(s) it refers to.**

_____

_____

> **Which line in the closing expresses the main idea of the composition?**

_____

_____

Conventions

Eduardo's sentences are put together correctly, and his usage, spelling, capitalization, and punctuation are correct.

2 Respond to the Theme of the Prompt

When you write a composition in response to a triplet on the TAKS writing assessment, you won't actually be answering a question about one of the reading selections or the visual representation. Instead, the prompt will give you a topic that reflects a theme common to all three pieces in the triplet.

Here are some examples:

1. Write a composition explaining what you can learn from the past.
2. Write a composition discussing whether your friends can be like family to you.
3. Write a composition telling why it is important to challenge yourself.
4. Write a composition describing what a community is and what makes your community special.

A Each example contains a key word following the word composition. The first of these key words is *explaining*. What are the other three?

1. **Write the other three key words here.**

_____ _____ _____

Many students are made anxious by key words like these when they are asked to write a composition. What is meant by *explaining*? Is it different from *discussing* or *describing*? Just what do you want me to do? How do you want me to do it?

In fact, there's not much difference among in these words when they appear in a prompt like the ones above. You could substitute the word *telling* for any one of the key words and come up with the same composition that meets the demands of the prompt.

When you write in response to a prompt like the ones above, here are some of the things you might do:

• describe what happens

• tell why something happens

• give reasons to support an opinion

What are some of the other things you might you do when you write to explain, or discuss, or tell about, or describe a topic?

_____

_____

_____

_____

_____

_____

B The remainder of each sample prompt is a statement of the theme—the big idea shared by the selections in the triplet. The theme in the first example could be restated this way:

What can people learn from the past?

1 **Restate the theme of the second example.**

_____

_____

2 **Restate the theme of the third example.**

_____

_____

3 **Restate the theme of the fourth example.**

_____

_____

C Before you begin to write your composition, there is one more step to take. Many of the details and examples in your composition will come from your own experience, so you need to find the ways in which you relate to the theme.

For instance, Jamella had a strong emotional response to the theme of learning from the past. When she started to brainstorm, she made three headings on her paper, with a few details and examples under each one:

How I Feel

—I'm very sure that this is important.

—I like knowing what others have done in various situations in the past.

What My Personal Experience Has Been

—My grandmother has always told me stories about the past.

—I use the past to guide me in everyday life.

—My grandmother's courage has been an example for me.

What I Know From Reading, Listening, Viewing, And Direct Observation

—My father listens to my grandmother's stories and draws lessons from them.

—My aunt tells stories from her childhood when she wants to make a point.

—In the short story "A Glorious Day," the main character changes a decision when he remembers something that happened during the war.

 Try Jamella's strategy for yourself. Here are the rest of the TAKS topics. Using Jamella's three headings, brainstorm details and examples from your own experience.

1 Write a composition discussing whether your friends can be like family to you.

How I Feel

_____

_____

_____

What My Personal Experience Has Been

_____

_____

_____

What I Know From Reading, Listening, Viewing And Direct Observation

_____

_____

_____

2   Write a composition explaining why it is important to challenge yourself.

How I Feel

_____

_____

_____

What My Personal Experience Has Been

_____

_____

_____

What I Know From Reading, Listening, Viewing And Direct Observation

_____

_____

_____

3   Write a composition describing what a community is and what makes your community special.

How I Feel

_____

_____

_____

What My Personal Experience Has Been

_____

_____

What I Know From Reading, Listening, Viewing And Direct Observation

_____

_____

_____

3 Writing a Good Opening

Carla is writing a composition about the importance of cutting down on the amount of stuff that we buy. Here is an example of an opening that Carla wrote in order to get her readers' attention and tell them what the paper is about:

> Can you imagine a mountain made up of millions of tons of trash—paper, cans, and bottles? It would be higher than our tallest buildings, and wider, too. It's hard to imagine; yet that's how much trash people in American create every year. For years, we've been burying it in landfills, but the landfills are getting full. Clearly, we need to cut down on the amount of trash we produce, or it will bury us.

Which sentence is the "grabber"—the one that gets your attention?

Write it here.

_____

_____

_____

_____

Which sentence tells you what the paper is about?

Write it here.

_____

_____

_____

A strong opening is an important element of a successful piece of writing. Make sure you hook your readers at the beginning of the paper. Tell them something that will make them want to go on reading. Then tell them what your main idea or topic is. Think of your opening as an advertisement for the rest of the composition.

Carla used a question as her "grabber." However, there are other effective ways of writing an opening for a composition.

BEGIN WITH ACTION

The tortured brakes squealed as the rear of the SUV skidded leftward on the hot pavement of Route 70 west of Plainview. The road curved off to the right. The vehicle didn't. It spun off the pavement at nearly eighty miles an hour.

Riding in the back seat was my cousin. He's in a wheelchair now. He's there because his friends thought that guzzling beer while driving wouldn't affect their reflexes.

Which sentence is the "grabber"—the one that gets your attention?

Write it here.

_____

_____

_____

Which sentence tells you what the paper is about?

Write it here.

_____

_____

_____

BEGIN WITH A STORY

Once a week, when all her classmates are at lunch in the cafeteria, Mary Hicks, a high school junior and honor student, walks down the block to the Brown Elementary School. Slipping into the first-grade classroom, she picks up a book and begins what she considers the most rewarding and exciting part of her week. She reads a story to a dozen wide-eyed children.

Mary is one of a growing number of students who are required to do volunteer work during the school year.

Which sentence is the "grabber"—the one that gets your attention?

Write it here.

_____

_____

Which sentence tells you what the paper is about?

Write it here.

_____

_____

_____

BEGIN WITH DIALOGUE

"Wait right there," says the student monitor at the front door of West Side High School. "I need to check your skirt length." Whipping out a tape measure, she kneels in front of Betsy Caldwell, a junior at West Side.

"Well, the rest of my outfit is OK," Betsy says defensively, smoothing the sleeves of her navy blazer and tucking the tails of her white shirt more tightly into the waistband of her skirt.

"The rest is up to code," the student monitor agrees, "and so is your skirt—but just. Another half an inch and I'd have to send you home to change."

This is becoming a common scene at West Side and other high schools around the state where students have created and are enforcing a dress code.

Which two sentences constitute the "grabber"—the ones that get your attention?

Write them here.

_____

_____

_____

Which sentence tells you what the paper is about?

Write it here.

_____

_____

_____

BEGIN WITH A DEFINITION

Recycling is a way of limiting the amount of trash we have to get rid of by finding other ways to use it. Sometimes, recycled items are used just as they are: milk containers, for instance, can be sterilized and refilled with milk. Other items are transformed in some way. Old paper is mashed up and turned into new, recycled paper. Recycling things instead of throwing them away isn't hard to do, and it has a positive impact on the environment.

Which sentence gets your attention with a definition?

Write it here.

_____

_____

_____

Which sentence tells you what the paper is about?

Write it here.

_____

_____

_____

What do these examples show about one way to structure a paragraph that opens with a grabber?

_____

_____

_____

_____

_____

_____

4 Add Relevant Examples

Even on a composition written for a test, you want to make your writing as lively and convincing as possible. One of the best ways is to use examples—bits of stories that illustrate your point and make it come alive for your readers. A good example draws readers into your paper. It gives them an action or event they can visualize and relate to. Instead of just reading **about** something, they can see it happening. With an example, you can **show** your readers what you mean instead of telling them.

This is the example Dennis added when he revised a paper on why it is important to be honest in school, even though it can be difficult at times:

> Last week, for instance, we had a test in social studies. I know it was going to be a tough test, but I was working after school and I had basketball practice. There just wasn't much time to study, and all my extracurricular stuff seemed more important than school. Of course, when I saw the test questions, the first thing I wanted to do was look around for help. It would have been easy to do. Mr. Peters was correcting last week's essays and not really looking at the class. Next to me, the best student in the class was filling up a page with her answers, in big, clear handwriting. I didn't cheat, but I could really see how easy it would be.

How is the example related to the subject of Dennis's paper?

_____

_____

_____

What point does Dennis illustrate with his example?

_____

_____

_____

For each of the following main ideas, write an example. Make sure your example tells a story that illustrates the main idea. To find good examples, think about your own experience—things that have happened to you or to friends, stories that you have read, or reports that you have seen on TV.

1. It is extremely dangerous to drink when you are going to be driving.

    _____

    _____

    _____

2. There are many benefits for you and others when you do volunteer work.

    _____

    _____

    _____

3. Without a dress code, students sometimes wear inappropriate clothes to school.

    _____

    _____

    _____

4. The things you learn in high school can be very helpful to you on the job.

    _____

    _____

    _____

5. Sometimes, being a high school student is like being a laboratory rat in a maze.

    _____

    _____

    _____

5 Incorporate Ideas from the Selections

You are not required to refer to ideas and information in the reading selections when you respond to a triplet on the TAKS 10 writing assessment. However, using the reading selections as a source of ideas is a good strategy, and may even help you improve your answer.

A   Jamella was preparing to answer the following question:

Write a composition explaining what you can learn from the past.

She thought about one of the reading selections in a triplet she had just read, a newspaper article headlined "Standing on the Shoulders of Giants." It was about local people whose role models were historical figures, such as the reformer Ida B. Wells and the folklorist-historian Américo Paredes. That article made her think about how she learned from the past. When she drafted her composition, she reread the following section of the article:

> *Historians sometimes say that those who fail to learn from history are doomed to repeat it. That suggests that history is a series of bad decisions and actions with tragic consequences. For some, though, history is a success story that provides inspiration for the present.*
>
> *Emma Culver, who recently became the principal of Crockett High School, is one of a number of people who draw strength from the past. She is attracted especially by the story of Ida B. Wells, the great African-American journalist and social reformer. "I first heard of Wells," she says, "when a librarian steered me to a biography of her. Before then, I had no notion that some of the ideas we associate with the Civil Rights movement were around so much earlier. And they were the ideas of a very independent and unusual woman! Reading about Wells made me determined to always stand up for my beliefs, even if they are unpopular ones."*

Then Jamella inserted this reference into her own composition:

> *As the article "Standing on the Shoulders of Giants" indicates, the past can give us important models for our behavior today.*

1.   Which statement in the text Jamella read supports the idea that history can provide role models for today?

_____

_____

_____

2.   Which statement in the text provides an example of how a historical figure became a role model for someone living today?

_____

_____

_____

B   Here is a second TAKS question:

Write a composition discussing whether your friends can be like a family to you.

Below is a section of a story from the triplet that preceded this question:

> "He's a weirdo," Kyle jeered. "Why do you hang out with him? He's such a loser, dude. Just dump him."
>
> Danny could feel his jaw tightening. Kyle was right. Leon was strange in every way—not just his name. Glancing at his friend, who had been backed into a corner by the taunting, threatening group, he could see it clearly. Leon was doing nothing to defend himself. He just seemed to pull down a shutter, closing himself off the way he usually did.
>
> Why don't you fight back? Danny wanted to scream. Why don't you show these guys what you're really like? At the same time, he wanted to say Who—him? What makes you think he's my friend?
>
> But they had known each other their whole lives, Danny and Leon. How could Danny desert him now? How could he explain his loyalty to Leon?
>
> "Hey," Danny said, stepping between Leon and Kyle. "I can't do that. He's kinda like a cousin."

Imagine that the main idea of the composition you are writing is that sometimes friends can be as close as family members. How would you make a reference to the story above? Use Jamella's statement in section A of this lesson as a model.

Write your statement here.

_____

_____

_____

_____

6 Find Your Own Voice

When your TAKS 10 composition is scored, one of the qualities the scorers will be looking for is voice. Voice is what makes your writing individual: it is the sound of your own voice.

Compare the two examples below.

Example 1. **You may never have heard of the people who are my role models. Their names don't appear in the news, and you won't see them on TV or in the movies. But to me, they're as interesting and important as the president of the United States or an NFL quarterback.**

Example 2. **I have several role models. They're not famous, but they're all unusual people.**

A How do the two examples compare?

1 Which example makes you more interested in finding out what the writer has to say?

_____

2 Which example gives you a better idea of what kind of person the writer is?

_____

B What gives the first example above its sense of voice? How does the writer express his or her individuality?

1 How does the writer tell you that his/her role models are not famous people?

_____

_____

_____

2 How does the writer tell you that these role models are unusual people?

_____

_____

_____

C Example 1 above is only one way to express the following idea:

My role models are not famous people, but they are all unusual.

How would you express this idea with your own voice? Write your own version. Let your personality and interests guide your choice of words. Use examples that are meaningful to you. And remember that what you write should sound like you.

Write your version here:

_____

_____

_____

_____

_____

D Using your own voice, rewrite each of the sentences below. Your rewritten version can be more than one sentence long.

1 Friends are good if you have a small family.

_____

_____

_____

2 People who don't challenge themselves never improve.

_____

_____

_____

3 A community can give you a sense of belonging.

_____

_____

_____

7 Connect Ideas

In order to make your ideas clear to your reader, you need to show how they are connected. Transition words like *also* or *in this case* or *first of all* are a simple way to connect ideas—and the one you are probably most familiar with. Experienced writers, though, make connections in a variety of other ways as well:

- by repeating words from one sentence to the next:

    In the **summer**, we have more free time. That's why **summer** is my favorite season.

- by using a word like *this* or *they* or *then* to refer to something in an earlier sentence:

    Summer is made for relaxing. Most people take their vacations then.

- by combining ideas into one sentence:

    A few weird people prefer winter **because** they would rather work or go to school than relax.

A   Here is an example from an essay Darrell wrote:

> *Community service provides extra help in places that can't afford to hire more people—for example, schools, libraries, hospitals, and nursing homes. It is dependent on volunteers, so requiring high school students to do community service sounds like a good idea. This experience would also benefit the students.*

1   In the second sentence, Darrell makes a connection by using the pronoun *it* to refer to something in the first sentence. What does *it* refer to? _____

2   In sentence 2, Darrell also repeats a phrase that occurs in sentence 1. What does he repeat? _____

3   Finally in sentence 2, Darrell combines two ideas. What word does he use to combine ideas? _____

4   In sentence 3, Darrell uses the phrase *this experience* to refer to something in sentence 2. What idea do these words refer to?

    _____

5   Sentence 3 also contains a transition word that connects this sentence to the ones preceding it. What transition word does Darrell use? _____

B For each item below, identify the ways in which Darrell connects ideas.

1   What is wrong with the idea of requiring high school students to do community service? For one thing, it is difficult to implement.

_____

2   Most volunteers do a better job if they have been trained, but training volunteers takes time and money.

_____

3   Volunteers also need to be supervised. Someone needs to make sure they show up on time and do their jobs correctly.

_____

4   Would the high school students do their volunteer work during school hours, or would they be expected to volunteer after school?

_____

5   Finally, how would the students get to their volunteer jobs? Most of them are too young to drive or don't have cars.

_____

C Rewrite the sentences below, adding words or combining ideas to make connections.

You need to come up with a plan. It has to be a plan that will work. You need to figure out how to make volunteer work appealing to high school students. You might want to give high school students credit. They would have a concrete reward for their efforts.

_____

_____

_____

_____

_____

_____

8 Edit As You Go

Your chances of doing well on the TAKS Test are increased if you revise and edit what you have written—that is, if you make sure that your writing obeys the conventions of written English. In the next lesson of this unit, you will have a chance to practice revising, and the entire next unit in this book is devoted to both editing and revising. Right now, you will be practicing editing—correcting spelling, punctuation, capitalization, and usage. To simplify the job of editing your completed draft, get into the habit of checking these things as you write.

Felicity has written a paragraph that is ready for editing. There are 10 errors in her paragraph. Make the corrections for her by crossing out anything that is wrong and writing in the correct form. Be prepared to explain your corrections. (Review the explanations in the Handbook.) The sentences are numbered to help you identify the location of your changes.

(1) This nation been producing trash and handing it over to someone else to dispose of. (2) Expecting that the problem will be solved. (3) Now its time for us to grow up and take care of our own garbage. (4) One way to get rid of trash is to burn it but many incinerators have had to be shut down because they violate the Clean air Act. (5) Incinerators can be improved however—some European countries have been incinerating their trash for more than 40 years and have developed a technology for burning waste cleanly and efficient. (6) Before we follow their lead, (7) our citizens would have to learn to seperate their garbage into things that can be burned and things that are non-burnable. (8) Right now, when certain plastics burn, the gases that are produced form poisonous compounds.

9 Revising a Composition

You have analyzed a good composition and practiced many of the strategies that will help you write your own. Now you will learn to apply what you have learned by revising someone else's writing, this time on a different topic.

Here is the prompt:

> **Write a composition that discusses what kind of role models are important for students to have while they are in school.**

Here is the essay that one student wrote in response to the prompt:

1   *Students need good role models. Everyone knows that role models are important. Some people in high school choose sports figures as role models. They should be careful about picking the right ones. Where do your role models come from? What do you learn from them?*

2   *The role model I learned the most from was Elvis Pritchard, my uncle. He was always there for me. Even when the rest of my family didn't understand me. For example, when he was a teenager, he goofed off and didn't study very hard. As a result, he didn't graduate with his peers. He worked in a garage and was good at fixing tractors, but he never got anywhere. Then he decided to go back to school and get his diploma and go on to community college. He learned how to repair computer parts in trucks and now makes a good living.*

3   *I learned from a sports figure, too. Bernie Williams is a great centerfielder for the New York Yankees. Although he is not a natural athlete, he is an asset to the team. He practices every day so that he can get better.*

4   *Finally, I have to say that my big sister is my guiding light. She always looks out for me, no matter what. I don't know what I'd do without her.*

Imagine that you wrote this essay and that you want to improve it. First, however, decide what you like about this essay so that you will remember to keep the parts you think are good.

Journal Entry: Making Connections

I want to keep _____

_____

_____

because _____

_____

_____

Now read each question below and think about how you would answer it. If you are working in a group, listen to what others have to say, and share your answers with them. Then write the changes you would make.

1   What is the main idea of the first paragraph? Does it have a single focus?

        Rewrite the opening to provide a single focus.

        _____

        _____

        _____

        _____

2   Is the opening of my essay interesting? Does it provide the reader with an interesting example?

        Add a short example that will fit in with the new paragraph you wrote.

        _____

        _____

        _____

        _____

3   What is the point of the story in paragraph 2?

Write a sentence or two that explains the significance of this story.

_____

_____

_____

_____

4   What is the main idea in paragraph 3? Do I know why I consider this player to be a good role model?

Write the additional sentence or sentences here.

_____

_____

_____

_____

5   What do I mean by "guiding light" in paragraph 4? What do I need to add to make it match the others?

Write the additional sentence or sentences here.

_____

_____

_____

_____

6   What kind of closing do I need?

Write the additional sentence or sentences here.

_____

_____

_____

_____

144

7   Is any of the language in my composition too vague or general? If so, which words or sentences do I need to change?

Write the additional sentence or sentences here.

_____

_____

_____

_____

8   Do I need to correct any of my spelling, punctuation, or capitalization? If so, which words or sentences do I need to change?

Write the additional sentence or sentences here.

_____

_____

_____

_____

10 Writing Your Own Essay

Here is the prompt that you have been working with for most of this chapter.

Write a composition that discusses what kind of role models are important for students to have while they are in school.

The information in the box below will help you remember what you should think about when you write your composition.

REMEMBER—YOU SHOULD

- write about the assigned topic
- make your writing thoughtful and interesting
- make sure that each sentence you write contributes to the composition as a whole
- make sure that your ideas are clear and easy for the reader to follow
- write about your ideas in depth so that the reader is able to develop a good understanding of what you are
- proofread your writing to correct errors in spelling, capitalization, punctuation, grammar, and sentence structure

11 Revising Your Essay

Reader's Response Sheet
A REVISE-AND-EDIT TOOL

**When you have finished writing, exchange papers with a partner.
As you read each other's answer, follow these steps:**

1.   Did the writer respond to the assignment?   ❑ Yes   ❑ No

    Did he or she give good examples?   ❑ Yes   ❑ No

    If you don't think so, explain:

    _____

    _____

2.   I liked _____

    because _____

    I also liked _____

    because _____

3.   I want to know more about _____

    _____

    I also want to know more about _____

    _____

4.   I don't understand _____

    _____

5.   Does the writer need to make changes in punctuation, spelling, capitalization, word choice, or sentence structure?   ❑ Yes   ❑ No

Use your partner's response to help you revise and improve your paper.

UNIT 3
Revising and Editing

After you have drafted and revised a piece of writing, there is one more step you need to take: you need to edit what you've written. That is, you need to correct errors in punctuation, capitalization, sentence construction, usage, and spelling. To see what a difference editing can make, look at these two versions of a passage from a student composition.

In the first version, all the underlined items are errors:

> There are many novels that have a young person <u>comeing</u> of age as the main theme. <u>Usally</u> in these kinds of novels, the main character starts out young and inexperienced<u>. But</u> ends up a mature adult. The <u>Novel</u> *The <u>red</u> Badge of Courage* by Stephen Crane seems to be just this kind of novel. The main character is Henry Fleming<u>. a</u> Civil <u>war</u> soldier. <u>He is naive at the beginning then he experiences battle and fear and at the end he feels like a man.</u> Some literary critics think that Henry does become a man because of what <u>hes</u> experienced. <u>Other's</u>, however, think that Crane is being ironic.

Here is the same passage after editing, with all the errors corrected:

> There are many novels that have a young person coming of age as the main theme. Usually in these kinds of novels, the main character starts out young and inexperienced but ends up a mature adult. The novel *The Red Badge of Courage* by Stephen Crane seems to be just this kind of novel. The main character is Henry Fleming, a Civil War soldier. He is naive at the beginning. Then he experiences battle and fear, and at the end he feels like a man. Some literary critics think that Henry does become a man because of what he's experienced. Others, however, think that Crane is being ironic.

This unit will give you practice in recognizing and correcting some of the errors students make most frequently in their compositions. In addition, it will prepare you for the Revising and Editing portion of the TAKS test.

1 Make Sure Your Sentences Are Complete — Correct Fragments

When you edit your writing, you can begin by looking at sentence construction. Make sure that your sentences are neither too short nor too long, and that they are put together correctly. Also, check to see that your sentences are complete—that you haven't written any fragments.

How can you recognize a fragment? First of all, you need to know what a sentence is. Sentences can be short or long, but each one states a **complete** idea:

> Olivia, Yolanda, Ricardo, and Darrell, who are all in the 10th grade, have just transferred here from Plainview High School.

This is a long and somewhat complex sentence. However, it expresses just one main idea. It is long and complex because the sentence is about four people and includes some details about them.

These sentences are shorter and simpler:

> Olivia is a student.

> Darrell transferred.

Even though they are short, these sentences are also complete. They are not fragments. Like the longer sentence above, each one expresses just one complete thought.

A **fragment**, though, is not complete, even though it may look like a sentence. It is a piece of a sentence that starts with a capital letter and ends with a period. Because fragments don't contain all the sentence parts needed for a complete sentence, they can be a major problem in your writing.

How can you tell when a group of words is a fragment? One way is to see whether it expresses a complete idea. If it is incomplete, it is a fragment, not a sentence. Here are some examples of fragments. Notice that each one sounds as though it should be connected to something else:

> After the weekend. [What happened after the weekend?]

> Because we had too much homework. [What happened because we had too much homework?]

> Running and skipping down the street. [Who was running and skipping down the street?]

Which of the following are fragments and which are sentences? Next to each one, write **F** for fragment or **S** for sentence.

_____ **1.** Have they arrived?

_____ **2.** Before noon.

_____ **3.** Kevin agreed.

_____ **4.** Letitia wanted to know who was taking the morning shift and who was going to work in the afternoon.

_____ **5.** Her cousin Felicity, her next-door neighbor Justin, and three of their friends who are visiting from out of town.

Another way to recognize a fragment is to look at the first word. Fragments often begin with connecting words like **because**, **before**, **after**, **when**, **until**, and **if**. Whenever you see one of these words, look to see what follows it. If there is a short group of words with a period at the end, it is probably a fragment:

Because I needed money.

After Luis left for home.

However, if there is a short group of words followed by a comma and then another group of words, it is probably a sentence:

Because I needed money, **I decided to look for a job**.

After Luis left for home, **we realized he had forgotten his jacket**.

It is usually easy to fix fragments that begin with connecting words. The group of words that will complete the thought is often right next to the fragment. You just need to connect the two:

Fragment: I opened my umbrella. **As soon as** it began to rain.

Sentence: I opened my umbrella **as soon as** it began to rain.

Sentence: **As soon as** it began to rain, I opened my umbrella.

NOTICE: Photocopying any part of this book is forbidden by law.

151

The following paragraph contains numerous fragments. On the lines below, rewrite the paragraph, correcting the fragments. Remember to look for ways to connect each fragment to another group of words.

James considered his position carefully. Before he made his decision. He was going to run for class president. Even though it would be a lot of work. He checked the student handbook carefully. To make sure he understood the complicated procedure outlined there. The first step was to submit a petition. With 75 signatures from students in his class. The petition had to be submitted to the Student Council. One month before the election. The Student Council members would count and check all the signatures. They would announce who was on the ballot. As soon as they finished this step. Then the campaign would begin.

_____

_____

_____

_____

_____

_____

_____

_____

_____

_____

_____

_____

2 Fix Run-On Sentences

There's nothing wrong with joining two sentences. In fact, it's often a good idea. But be careful not to accidentally create a run-on sentence. A run-on occurs when you connect two sentences by just sticking them together, with no punctuation or connecting words between them, or with the wrong kind of punctuation. These are run-ons:

> Jason didn't complete his homework neither did Crystal.

> He didn't forget what he had learned, he just didn't know how to solve the problem.

Notice that if you read these two examples out loud, they sound perfectly fine. That's because you automatically supply a pause in the place where each pair of sentences has been joined. It's only when you write that they become run-on sentences.

Reading your sentences out loud is a good way to detect a run-on. If you hear a pause in the middle of a long sentence, check to see what you've written. If you don't see any punctuation or connecting words, or if you see only a comma, you've probably written a run-on.

Fortunately, a run-on is easy to correct once you've identified it:

- You can use a **comma** and a **connecting word:**

  Jason didn't complete his homework, **and** neither did Crystal.

  He didn't forget, **but** he just didn't know how to solve the problem.

- You can use a **semicolon:**

  Jason didn't complete his homework; neither did Crystal.

  He didn't forget; he just didn't know how to solve the problem.

- You can separate the two joined sentences and **let each one stand on its own:**

  Jason didn't complete his homework. **N**either did Crystal.

  He didn't forget. **H**e just didn't know how to solve the problem.

Rewrite the following paragraph. Correct the run-ons by adding the appropriate punctuation and/or connecting words.

Homework wasn't usually a problem for Crystal she did it as soon as she got home from school. This was a habit she had developed in grade school, her mother insisted on doing homework right away. After a while she began to see the advantage of this approach, she never had to worry about getting her assignments done on time. Then she was free to enjoy the rest of the day there was nothing else she had to do. Also, her mother never had to nag her, she knew that Crystal's homework would be done before she watched TV or went out with her friends.

_____

_____

_____

_____

_____

_____

_____

_____

_____

_____

_____

_____

_____

3 Combine Short Sentences—Use Transitions

Short sentences are not incorrect, but your writing will be much smoother and more interesting to read if you have a mixture of short and long sentences. One way to write longer sentences is to combine some of your short sentences.

Combining sentences can improve your writing in other ways as well. As you have already seen, it can help you avoid or correct fragments. Sentence combining is also a good way to show how your ideas are connected.

Here are some of the ways you can combine two or more short sentences.

✏ Use a connecting word like *and* or *but* to join either whole sentences or parts of sentences:

Uncombined:	We need candidates for president. We need candidates for secretary. We also need candidates for treasurer.
Combined:	We need candidates for president, secretary, **and** treasurer. We need candidates for president and secretary, **as well as** for treasurer.
Uncombined:	Maria has 75 names on her petition. Julia still needs 5 more names.
Combined:	Maria has 75 names on her petition, **but** Julia still needs 5 more names.

✏ Use a word like *when, although, if, because, before,* or *after* to join two sentences. Choose the connecting word carefully: it tells how the ideas in the two sentences are related.

The candidates turn in their petitions. The campaign begins.

The campaign begins **after** the candidates turn in their petitions.

Julia wanted to be a candidate. She didn't have enough names on her petition.

Although Julia wanted to be a candidate, she didn't have enough names on her petition.

✏ Use a word like **who**, **which**, or **that** to combine two sentences.

I am supporting Kevin. Kevin is running for class president.

I am supporting Kevin, **who** is running for class president.

Kevin thought of a campaign slogan. I like the slogan.

I like the campaign slogan **that** Kevin thought of.

✏ Make one sentence part of the other without adding any extra words. In fact, with this method you usually take out repeated words.

Tasha plans to vote for Kevin. Kevin is her cousin.

Tasha plans to vote for her cousin Kevin.

She heard Kevin today. He was making a speech in an assembly.

She heard Kevin making a speech in an assembly today.

In the following paragraph, find five places to make new, longer sentences by combining two or more short sentences. Then rewrite the paragraph, using the combining techniques shown in this lesson.

K. J. was the ninth-grade class secretary. He didn't want to run for an office in tenth grade. He finished his term last June. He wasn't interested in taking on that much responsibility again. He was exhausted. He had to attend a meeting every month. He had to take notes. He also had to write up the minutes. Writing the minutes took the longest. The minutes are a description of what happened in the meeting. K. J. is now the ex-secretary. He is looking forward to playing soccer again.

_____

_____

_____

_____

_____

_____

_____

_____

_____

6 Proofread for Capitalization, Apostrophes, and Spelling

When you have done all your other editing, you are ready to proofread. You are going to read everything carefully again, looking for errors in spelling, punctuation, and so on. Some of these errors occur because you're writing quickly and thinking more about the content than about commas and spelling. You may also make some errors because you aren't sure of the rules. (To help you, the rules are reviewed in the next unit of this book.)

So that you can focus on each word and mark of punctuation, this book provides two lessons on proofreading. Each one deals with a different group of errors that you may need to identify and correct in your own writing.

Capitalization

Here are some of the errors you might make in capitalization.

✏ You might forget to capitalize the first letter of a proper noun. This is an error that frequently occurs when the name of a place, an organization, or a holiday has more than one word in it:

Incorrect:	We went to South Padre island on our vacation.
Correct:	We went to South Padre **Island** on our vacation.
Incorrect:	Memorial day is always a Monday holiday.
Correct:	Memorial **Day** is always a Monday holiday.
Incorrect:	The Metropolitan transit Authority runs the city buses.
Correct:	The Metropolitan **Transit** Authority runs the city buses.

✏ You might forget to capitalize the first word in a direct quotation:

Incorrect:	Imogene shook hands and said, "it's so nice to meet you."
Correct:	Imogene shook hands and said, "**It's** so nice to meet you."

✏ You might forget to capitalize a word like *aunt, uncle, governor,* or *senator* when it's used with a name:

Incorrect:	Shaun invited aunt Joyce to go to the movies with him.
Correct:	Shaun invited **Aunt** Joyce to go to the movies with him.
Incorrect:	She went to hear representative O'Farrell speak instead.
Correct:	She went to hear **Representative** O'Farrell speak instead.

✏ You might capitalize a word that should not be capitalized.

Incorrect:	Joyce is my Aunt.
Correct:	Joyce is my **aunt**.
Incorrect:	The Fourth of July was the hottest day of the Summer.
Correct:	The Fourth of July was the hottest day of the **summer**.

Apostrophes

Here are some of the errors you might make in the use of **apostrophes**.

✏ You might leave out an apostrophe that you need, or you might put an apostrophe in the wrong place.

Incorrect:	Mario didnt remember to turn off the oven.
Incorrect:	Mario did'nt remember to turn off the oven.
Correct:	Mario **didn't** remember to turn off the oven.

✏ You might put in an apostrophe that you don't need.

Incorrect:	Felicity say's that book is her's.
Correct:	Felicity **says** that book is **hers**.

Spelling

You might also make spelling errors like these.

✏ You might double a letter that shouldn't be doubled.

biTTing, wriTTer, joKKed

✏ You might forget to double a letter that should be doubled.

wriTen, geTing, speLer

✏ You might forget to drop the final "e" when you add "-ing" to a word:

hopEing, bakEing, jokEing

✏ You might spell a vowel sound incorrectly.

rEson, mAbe, tickIt

✏ You might spell a consonant sound incorrectly.

Riting, Nife, neFew

✏ You might confuse words that sound alike but are spelled differently.

you're, your; they're, their, there

✏ You might reverse two letters.

thIEr, frEInd, recIEve

The following paragraph is from the first draft of a student report. There are 15 mistakes in capitalization, apostrophes, and spelling. Proofread to find each mistake, and correct it right on the draft. Cross out the words and letters you want to eliminate. Use a caret (^) to insert new words and letters. Write your corrections in the space above the incorrect words.

The Rio grande Valley is the part of Texas just north of the River

that seperates Texas from Mexico. When poeple figured out how to control

the flooding of the river, around the end of the ninteenth century, the

resident's were finaly able to farm, growing a variety of fruits and

vegetables their. The wheather in the area isnt as extreme as in some

other parts of the state, so it attracts winter visiters to. My uncle Joe is a

good example. Arriveing in a

recreational vehicle, he and my Aunt

pull into their favorite RV park and look

forward to weeks of outdoor activities.

7 Proofread for Punctuation and Usage

You've already seen, in the lessons on fragments and run-ons, how important punctuation can be. You need to check punctuation carefully when you proofread, both to avoid making errors and to make your meaning clearer. You also need to identify and correct errors in usage—that is, in the form of words like verbs and pronouns. Remember that the next unit of this book reviews the rules for you.

Punctuation

Here are some punctuation errors you might make when you write.

✏ Even though you know now that run-on sentences are incorrect, you still might forget to punctuate correctly when you join two sentences together.

Incorrect:	Mr. Carter recommended this book it's about a brother and sister growing up in a small southern town.
Incorrect:	Mr. Carter recommended this book, it's about a brother and sister growing up in a small southern town.

You can correct run-ons by using more than a comma to separate the two joined sentences. You can do this by using a semicolon between the two sentences, by using a comma and a connecting word, or by separating the two sentences completely.

Correct:	Mr. Carter recommended this book; it's about a brother and sister growing up in a small southern town.
Correct:	Mr. Carter recommended this book, which is about a brother and sister growing up in a small southern town.
Correct:	Mr. Carter recommended this book. It's about a brother and sister growing up in a small southern town.

✏ You might also forget that a group of words needs to express a complete thought if you are going to punctuate it as a sentence. If you put a period at the end of a group of words that is not complete enough to be a sentence, you have created a **fragment**. You can correct a fragment by joining it to another group of words to make a sentence.

Incorrect:	They live with their father. Who is a lawyer named Atticus.
Correct:	They live with their father, who is a lawyer named Atticus.

✏ You might forget that you need a comma (in addition to a connecting word) between two sentences that have been joined with a word like and or but.

Incorrect:	The boy in this story is named Jem and his sister's name is Scout.
Correct:	The boy in this story is named Jem, and his sister's name is Scout.

✏ You might forget that you need a comma between items in a series of three or more things.

Incorrect:	We have read novels by southern writers western writers and southwestern writers.
Correct:	We have read novels by southern writers, western writers, and southwestern writers.

✏ You might forget that you need a comma after an introductory phrase or clause.

Incorrect:	Naturally curious and adventurous Scout manages to get into trouble.
Correct:	Naturally curious and adventurous, Scout manages to get into trouble.
Incorrect:	Because their mother is dead Atticus is raising Jem and Scout alone.
Correct:	Because their mother is dead, Atticus is raising Jem and Scout alone.

Usage

Some words—especially pronouns and verbs—change form depending on how they are used in a sentence. You can make errors in usage when you are not sure which form of a word is correct—whether you should use him or he, for example, or whether sang or sung is correct.

✏ You might use the wrong form of a pronoun.

Incorrect:	Me and Sara asked Mr. Carter to recommend another book.
Correct:	Sara and I asked Mr. Carter to recommend another book.
Incorrect:	Mr. Carter asked Sara and I to tell the class about this book.
Correct:	Mr. Carter asked Sara and me to tell the class about this book.

✏ You might use the wrong form of a verb, especially in the past tense.

Incorrect:	Mr. Carter given us the best grade in the class.
Correct:	Mr. Carter gave us the best grade in the class.
Correct:	Mr. Carter has given us the best grade in the class.
Incorrect:	I done just as well in all my classes this year.
Correct:	I did just as well in all my classes this year.
Correct:	I have done just as well in all my classes this year.

Terrie wrote the following draft as part of an essay on Harper Lee's *To Kill a Mockingbird*. Proofread Terrie's draft carefully, and correct the errors in punctuation and usage. Again, cross out the words and letters you want to eliminate. Use a caret (^) to insert new words and letters. Write your corrections in the space above the incorrect words.

Although she never written another novel Harper Lee is still considered an important writer. Carson McCullers Flannery O'Connor and Harper Lee are often grouped together. As major southern women writers. They were all from the deep South and they all set many of their stories and novels in the South as well. Most of their work was done in the middle of the twentieth century. Harper Lee was a more popular writer than the other two, her book is on the reading list at many schools. Besides being a best-selling novel <u>To Kill a Mockingbird</u> was also made into a successful movie. The movie is very good and was gave many awards. Seeing <u>To Kill a Mockingbird</u> is how me and my family discovered the books of Harper Lee, McCullers, and O'Connor.

8 TAKS Editing Practice 1

The TAKS test uses a multiple-choice format to test you on revising and editing. This lesson and the one following will give you practice on this test format.

This composition was written by Georgia, a tenth grade student from Plano. She wrote it as part of a project on the history of her hometown. Help improve the project by reading Georgia's composition carefully and answering the questions that follow it.

Plano's Very Different Past

[1] Here in Plano, we used to streets with traffic lights and a steady stream of cars, buses, and trucks. [2] But once, this town was more rural than urban. [3] The sounds that filled the streets were more likely to be the clip-clopping of horse's than the blast of car horns.

[4] I spoke to Catherine McElroy. [5] She was born here in 1915. [6] She has lived here all her life. [7] She has observed many changes. [8] From her parents' stories, Ms. McElroy also knows what the town was like before her time. [9] She can tell you the history of every house in her neighborhood. [10] When it was built, who lived there, what kind of businesses they operated, even what they grew in their gardens.

[11] For example, the house at 901 East 18th Street used to be the Olney Davis House. [12] It looked much the way it does now, but the porch columns were added in a later addition. [13] Instead of being an office building, the house was lived in by one family. [14] The owner a prominent businessman named Olney Davis was the first president of the Plano schools' Board of Trustees. [15] Davis was also mayor of Plano at one time. [16] It didn't become an office building until the 1980s.

[17] Life here began to change after World War I, but it was World War II that brought the really big changes. [18] New highways made it easier for people to travel from here to Dallas, and nearly everyone could afford a car, too. [19] Farmers could make more money selling their land to builders than raising livestock, and so Plano became a suburb.

[20] The house Ms. McElroy lives in was built by her parents. [21] They had a small farm here, where they grew tomatoes, corn, cucumbers, and green beans. [22] Most of their produce was sold to stores in the city. [23] It was not an easy life, Ms. McElroy says, but she enjoyed the quiet and the clean, fresh air. [24] People out here had gardens of their own and didn't need to buy vegetables. [25] Plano is not so quiet today, but we do have an easier life.

1   What change, if any, should be made in sentence 1?

   A   Delete the comma after **Plano**

   B   Insert the word **are** after **we**

   C   Change **stream** to **streams**

   D   Make no change

2   What change, if any, should be made in sentence 3?

   A   Change **filled** to **had filled**

   B   Change **more likely** to **more likelier**

   C   Change **horse's** to **horses**

   D   Make no change

3   Which of these sentences could be added to the beginning of the second paragraph (sentences 4–9) to introduce the ideas in that paragraph?

   A   People who have lived in Plano for a long time can tell us what the town used to be like.

   B   Catherine McElroy is a very interesting person.

   C   My parents moved to Plano from Dallas before I was born.

   D   I was told I could improve my essay if I conducted interviews.

4   What is the most effective way to combine sentences 5, 6, and 7?

   A   Born here in 1915 and living here all her life, she has observed many changes.

   B   She has lived here all her life, after being born here in 1905, and has observed many changes.

   C   She was born here in 1915 and has observed many changes, being a lifelong resident.

   D   Born here in 1915, this lifelong resident has observed many changes.

5 What is the most effective way to rewrite the ideas in sentences 9 and 10?

A When each house was built, who lived in the neighborhood, what grew in their gardens—she can tell you the history of every house and every kind of business in town.

B She can tell you the history of every house in her neighborhood, including when it was built, who lived there, what kinds of businesses they operated, and even what they grew in their gardens.

C She told me when her house was built, who lived there, what kinds of business they operated, even what they grew in their garden— all of the history.

D She can tell you about each house in her neighborhood, including when it was built, who lives there, what kinds of businesses they operate, even what they grow in their gardens.

6 What change should be made in sentence 14?

A Change **owner** to **owners**

B Insert a comma after **owner**

C Insert commas after **owner** and **Davis**

D Change **Board of Trustees** to **board of trustees**

7 The meaning of sentence 16 can be clarified by changing It to —

A The family

B The house

C Olney Davis

D The Board of Trustees

8 What change, if any, should be made in sentence 18?

A Change **highways** to **highway's**

B Change **people** to **peoples**

C Change **too** to **to**

D Make no change

9 What is the most effective way to improve the organization of the final paragraph (sentences 20–25)?

A Move sentence 24 to between sentences 22 and 23.

B Move sentence 23 to the end of the paragraph.

C Move sentence 22 between sentences 20 and 21.

D Move sentence 25 to the beginning of the paragraph.

10 What change should be made in sentence 25?

A Change **is** to **are**

B Delete the word **but**

C Change **do** to **does**

D Change **easyer** to **easier**

9 TAKS Editing Practice 2

Hector wrote this essay for his tenth-grade home economics class. To help Hector show his readers how to shop more intelligently, read his essay carefully and answer the questions that follow it.

How To Be a Smart Shopper

[1] Smart shoppers know how to shop. [2] They know what isn't worth buying and what is. [3] They look for ways to save, and they knew how to recognize sales that aren't really bargains. [4] If you want to be a smart shopper the first thing to learn is where to shop.

[5] There are so many different kinds of stores to choose from! [6] Large supermarkets carry many different kinds of food in many brands and sizes. [7] Their prices are usually lower than at other stores. [8] What kinds of stores do smart shoppers shop at? [9] Another type convenience stores are just what their name says they are. [10] They don't carry as many brands and sizes, and their prices are higher. [11] They are open more hours of the day, and they are usually near your house.

[12] If you have two supermarkets in your neighborhood, you will need to find out which one has the best prices. [13] Find at each store prices you are likely to buy for a number of items. [14] Take this list with you: ground beef, chicken, eggs, milk, bananas, bread, and orange juice. [15] Then write down the cost of each item at each store, add the figures up, and compare.

[16] Picking a supermarket is just the first step buying wisely is the next. [17] Look for the items that are on sale each week. [18] Even when something is on sale. [19] Compare the price with another brand. [20] Is the sale item still cheaper? [21] When you do see a good bargain, stock up for weeks ahead. [22] But remember that buying a large quantity of something no one likes is never a bargain.

[23] Smart shopping may seem like a waste of valuable time. [24] But if you take the time to shop wisely, you will find that the savings quickly add up. [25] Smart shoppers soon find themselves with extra money to spend on special gifts or a family vacation.

1   What change should be made in sentence 3?

   A   Change **look** to **looking**

   B   Change **knew** to **know**

   C   Change **aren't** to **weren't**

   D   Change **really** to **real**

2   What change, if any, should be made in sentence 4?

   A   Insert a comma after **shopper**

   B   Insert a comma after **thing**

   C   Insert a comma after **learn**

   D   Make no change

3   What is the most effective way to improve the organization of the second paragraph (sentences 5-11)?

   A   Move sentence 5 between sentences 8 and 9

   B   Move sentence 8 to the beginning of the paragraph

   C   Move sentence 10 to the end of the paragraph

   D   Delete sentence 11

4   What change should be made in sentence 9?

   A   Delete the word **type**

   B   Insert commas after **type** and **stores**

   C   Change **their** to **there**

   D   Change **says** to **say**

5   What transition should be added to the beginning of sentence 11?

   A   Besides,

   B   Furthermore,

   C   However,

   D   Nonetheless,

6   What change, if any, should be made in sentence 12?

   A   Insert a comma after **supermarkets**

   B   Change **neighborhood** to **nieghborhood**

   C   Replace the comma after **neighborhood** with a semicolon

   D   Make no change

NOTICE: Photocopying any part of this book is forbidden by law.

171

7 What is the most effective way to rewrite sentence 13?

A At each store, find prices for a number of items you are likely to buy.

B Find a number of items at each store you are likely to buy.

C Find you are likely to buy a number of items at each store for prices.

D For a number of items, find prices you are likely to buy at each store.

8 What change should be made in sentence 16?

A Change **Picking** to **Pick**

B Insert a semicolon after **step**

C Insert a comma after **step**

D Delete the word **the**

9 What is the most effective way to rewrite the ideas in sentences 18 and 19?

A Even when something is on sale, and compare the price with another brand.

B Even when something is on sale; however, compare the price with another brand.

C Even when something is on sale; compare the price with another brand.

D Even when something is on sale, compare the price with another brand.

10 Which of these sentences could be added to the end of the final paragraph (sentences 23–25) to support the ideas in that paragraph?

A New stereos, new televisions, and even a new car can be purchased with your savings, that is, if you buy enough things.

B If you take notes on what your family eats, you won't have to worry about buying things no one likes.

C Then, no one will think that smart shopping is a waste!

D A family vacation can bring parents and children closer together.

FEEDBACK AND COACHING TIPS
Editing Practice Selection 1—Plano's Very Different Past

1. Choice **A** is incorrect because *Here in Plano* is an introductory phrase that should be separated from the rest of the sentence with a comma. Choice B is also incorrect because the article *a* indicates that *stream* should stay singular. A change does need to be made in sentence 1, however, so choice D is incorrect. The auxiliary verb *are* needs to be added to used. The correct answer is choice **C**.

2. The correct answer is choice **C**. *Horse's* is the possessive form of the noun *horse*, and the plural form horses—no apostrophe—is needed here. Don't put an apostrophe in a plural unless it's a plural possessive! Choice A is incorrect because it makes an unnecessary change in the form of the verb—the past tense filled matches sentence 3. Choice B is incorrect because *more likelier* is an example of nonstandard usage. Finally, because a change is needed, choice D is also incorrect.

Tip from the Coach

When a question asks you to add a sentence to a paragraph, read the paragraph and all four choices before answering. If you're choosing a first sentence for the paragraph, it should introduce the main idea.

3. Choice B is related to the material in the paragraph—it mentions Catherine McElroy—but it does not introduce the paragraph's main point. Choices C and D have little or nothing to do with this paragraph. The correct answer is choice **A**. This sentence introduces the paragraph's most important ideas.

4. Sentences 5, 6, and 7 each state a basic fact about Ms. McElroy, and they can be smoothly combined into one sentence. Choice D makes sentence 7 the main part of the sentence, turning sentence 5 into an introductory phrase and sentence 6 into a modifier. Choice **D** is the correct answer. Choices A, B, and C are all awkward and choppy.

5. Choice **B** is the correct answer. It combines sentences 9 and 10—a sentence fragment—into one grammatically correct sentence with the original meaning. Choices A, C, and D are all grammatically correct sentences, but in each one the original meaning is changed. All three are incorrect.

Tip from the Coach

When a question asks for the most effective way to combine sentences, more than one choice may be grammatically correct. The correct choice must also be well written and have the exact same meaning as the original sentences.

6. Choice A is incorrect. Sentence 14 refers to only one owner, so the word *owner* should not be made plural. Choice D is incorrect also, because *Board of Trustees* should be capitalized. A comma should be added after *owner*, but this is not the only comma needed—so choice B is also incorrect. The phrase *a prominent businessman named Olney Davis* is an appositive that should be set off by **two** commas. The correct answer is choice **C**.

7. Choice **B** is the correct answer. The antecedent of the pronoun *It* is the *house*. Neither choice A, choice C, nor choice D is the correct antecedent. Furthermore, choice C does not agree with the pronoun It.

Tip from the Coach

When a question asks you to clarify a sentence's meaning by changing a pronoun, read the whole paragraph carefully to find out which choice makes the most sense.

8. Choice A is incorrect. The subject of sentence 18, *highways*, is a plural noun and should not be changed to a singular possessive form. Choice B is also incorrect. *People* is the correct plural form of this noun. The word *too*—meaning "as well as"—is spelled correctly, so choice C is also wrong. The correct answer is choice **D**. No change should be made in sentence 18.

9. Choice **A** is the correct answer. Sentence 24 is out of place, and the paragraph would be better organized if it was moved between sentences 22 and 23. Choices B, C, and D are all incorrect. Each of these changes would actually make the paragraph less organized.

Tip from the Coach

When a question asks you to improve the organization of a paragraph, read the paragraph carefully to find any sentences that seem to be in the wrong place. If a sentence is relevant but confusing, it may need to be moved.

10. The verbs *is* and *does* both agree with their subjects and should not be changed. Choices A and C are incorrect. The conjunction *but* is needed in this sentence; without it, there would be a run-on sentence. Choice B is also incorrect. The correct answer is choice **D**. When *-er* is added to the word *easy* to form the comparative, the letter *y* is changed to the letter *i*.

Editing Practice Selection 2—How to Be a Smart Shopper

1. Choice A is incorrect because *looking* would be a nonstandard usage in sentence 3. Choice D is also incorrect. Changing *really* to *real* would not create a grammatical error, but it would not correct one, either. Choice C, changing the present tense verb aren't to the past tense *weren't*, would make this verb match the tense of *knew*. However, the first part of this compound sentence is in the present tense. *Knew* should be changed to the present tense *know*. The correct answer is choice **B**.

2. The correct answer is choice **A**. *If you want to be a smart shopper* is a dependent clause and should be separated from the rest of the sentence with a comma. Choices B and C both insert the comma within sentence 4's independent clause, so they are both incorrect. Because a comma is needed, choice D is also incorrect.

3. Choices A and C are both incorrect. Moving these sentences will not improve the second paragraph's organization and may even make it less effective. Choice C is also incorrect. Although sentence 11 may not seem as relevant as sentence 10, for example, removing it will not improve the paragraph's organization. The best choice is **B**. Sentence 8 introduces the main idea and should come at the paragraph's beginning.

Tip from the Coach

When a question asks you to improve the organization of a paragraph, read the paragraph carefully to find any sentences that seem to be in the wrong place. If a sentence is relevant but confusing, it may need to be moved.

4. The correct answer is choice **B**. *Convenience stores* is an appositive—it modifies *type*—and should be separated from the rest of the sentence with commas. Choice A is incorrect because the word *type* is needed in sentence 9. *Their*, the plural possessive pronoun, is the correct word in sentence 9, so choice C is also incorrect. Choice D is incorrect as well. The verb form *says* agrees with its subject.

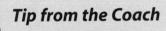

Tip from the Coach

A transition helps readers move smoothly from one idea to the next. When a question asks you for a transition, look closely at both of the sentences it will connect and choose the transition that makes the most sense.

5. Both choice A and choice B would be used to connect examples that support the same point. But the facts described in sentence 11 do not support the same point as the facts in sentence 10, though, so these choices are incorrect. Choice D would not make sense between sentences 10 and 11 either, so it is also incorrect. *However* is the appropriate transition between sentences 10 and 11. The correct answer is choice **C**.

6. Choice A is incorrect. *In your neighborhood* is not an appositive and should not be set apart with commas. *Neighborhood* is spelled correctly, so choice B is also incorrect. Choice C is incorrect as well. The first part of sentence 12 is a dependent clause; it should be joined to the second part with a comma, not a semicolon. In fact, no changes should be made in sentence 12. Choice **D** is the correct answer.

Tip from the Coach

When a question asks you to choose the most effective way to rewrite a sentence, the answer will have the original sentence's meaning and no grammatical errors.

7. Neither of the sentences in choices C and D makes sense, so these choices are incorrect. Choice B, on the other hand, does make sense—but it leaves out significant words from the original sentence 13, and its meaning does not fit the paragraph. The correct answer is choice **A**. The misplaced modifiers in the original sentence 13 now modify the correct words.

8. The correct answer is choice **B**. Sentence 16 is a run-on sentence, and because there is no conjunction, the two independent clauses need to be joined with a semicolon. Choice C is incorrect because it would create a run-on sentence. *Picking* is the correct word form for sentence 16, so choice A is incorrect. Choice D is also incorrect. While deleting *the* would not create an error, it would leave sentence 16 a run-on.

Tip from the Coach

When a question asks you to correct a run-on, pay close attention to the connection between the two parts of the sentence. Are they both independent clauses, or is one dependent? Is there conjunction or a transitional word?

9. Sentence 18 is a sentence fragment—a dependent clause that needs to be combined with the independent clause in sentence 19. Choices A, B, and C combine sentences 18 and 19 in ways that are correct for combining two independent clauses. But none of these are correct ways to combine a dependent and an independent clause, so all three choices are incorrect. The correct answer is choice **D**. A simple comma combines the sentences.

Tip from the Coach

When a question asks for the most effective way to combine sentences, more than one choice may be grammatically correct. The correct choice must also be well written and have the exact same meaning as the original sentences.

10. Choices B and D both refer to ideas in the final paragraph, but neither one supports the paragraph's main idea. Both choices are incorrect. Choice A supports the ideas of the *previous* paragraph, so it is also incorrect. (And the statement that it makes is pretty ridiculous.) The correct answer is choice **C**. Only this sentence supports and ties together the ideas in the final paragraph.

Tip from the Coach

When a question asks you to add a sentence to a paragraph, read the paragraph and all four choices before answering. If you're choosing a final sentence for the paragraph, it should tie the paragraph's ideas together.

APPENDIX
Writer's Handbook
of Punctuation, Capitalization, Usage, Sentence Construction, and Spelling

Your writing is not complete if you haven't edited it to remove mistakes in punctuation, capitalization, usage, grammar, sentence construction, or spelling—all the topics reviewed in this chapter. These topics are often grouped together and called **conventions of standard English**.

To give you an idea of what errors in the conventions of standard English can do to a composition, look at this passage, which you read earlier. All the items in boldface (black) type are errors. They make a mess of an otherwise acceptable piece of writing.

> Navajo **coad** talkers started sending their **coad messiges**. They **start** only nine months after the war started. The idea **comes** from Philip Johnson. **An** engineer who **work** for the city of **los angeles**. Johnson was the son of a **mishunnary** who lived on the Navajo **reservation** in **new** Mexico and **arizona**. He had **growed** up **speeking navajo** with his Navajo playmates **he** was at that time one of the very few non-Navajos in the world. **Who** could understand their language?

Here is the same passage, edited, with all corrections made.

> Navajo code talkers started sending their code messages only nine months after the war started. The idea came from Philip Johnson, an engineer who worked for the city of Los Angeles. Johnson was the son of a missionary who lived on the Navajo Reservation in New Mexico and Arizona. He had grown up speaking Navajo with his Navajo playmates, and he was at that time one of the very few non-Navajos in the world who could understand their language.

This chapter will review some of the most common errors that students make in their compositions.

Punctuation and Capitalization

1. End Markers

Period

1.1   A period marks the end of a sentence.

Rhonda just shrugged her shoulders and laughed.

1.2   A period marks the end of an abbreviation.

Mr.   Mrs.   Ms.   Dr.   Lt. (Lieutenant)

Gen. (General)   Tx. (Texas)   Mt. (Mount)

EXCEPTION: Miss

Question Mark

1.3   A question mark goes at the end of a question.

Why don't you try the gumbo?

1.4   Do *not* use a question mark after an indirect quotation. Use a period.

Mark asked Luisa why she didn't try the gumbo.

Exclamation Mark or Exclamation Point

1.5   An exclamation point goes at the end of a sentence expressing strong emotion.

I'm sick and tired of listening to your complaints!

1.6   An exclamation point goes at the end of a strong command.

Stop!   Don't you dare do that!

1.7   An exclamation point goes after certain kinds of expressions beginning with what or how that are *not* questions.

What a thoughtful thing to do!

How easy it is to make dumb mistakes!

PRACTICE

Punctuate these sentences correctly by adding punctuation where needed.

1   Get out of here

2   Dr. Vernon wants to know when Miss Jessie is coming back

3   Is she coming back at all

4   What a strange question that is

5   What else does he want to know

2. Commas

The comma rules on this page deal with placing a comma between items in series—that is, like a list.) Use commas—

2.1   In a series of three or more words, phrases, or clauses, between each member of the series. (The last comma is optional.)

> *Words:* **Florida, Louisiana, and Texas** all border on the Gulf of Mexico.

> *Phrases:* June stormed **down the stairs, out the door, and into the street**.

> *Clauses:* We don't know **who he is, where he came from, or why he is here**.

2.2   Between certain adjectives, if you could use the word and between them instead of the comma.

> a warm, comfortable bed   a clear, cold, sunny morning

But if the word and would not sound natural, do NOT put in a comma.

> a tall brick building   curly brown hair

2.3   Between independent clauses—clauses that can be sentences by themselves— before any of these "coordinating" conjunctions.

> *and   but   or   nor   yet   for*

> Rodney objected, **but** no one paid any attention.

But do *not* put a comma in a sentence like this:

> Benny grunted and groaned but couldn't lift the box.

Here, the conjunctions *and* and *but* do not join independent clauses. They join verbs. (That is, if what comes after the conjunction would not be a sentence by itself, don't put in a comma.)

> **Wrong:**   Jean slammed the window down, and fell back into her chair.

> **Correct:**   Jean slammed the window down and fell back into her chair.

NOTICE: Photocopying any part of this book is forbidden by law.

179

PRACTICE

Punctuate these sentences correctly by adding commas where needed.

1. We saw Mae and Deb but Fred Mark and Ben were nowhere in sight.

2. A cold damp wind whistled through the cracks of the little old house.

3. Jack shook his head turned and walked out the door.

4. Jack just shook his head and walked out the door.

5. Jack just shook his head but Bruce turned and walked out the door.

The comma rules on this page deal with items that are set off by commas, that is, that have a comma both before and after them. (Of course, if one of these items begins or ends a sentence, only one comma is possible.)

Use commas—

2.4 To set off appositives. An appositive is a noun (plus any other words that describe or modify it) that stands next to another noun and gives additional information about it.

> Redwoods, **the tallest trees in the world**, grow near the California coast.

2.5 To set off non-restrictive (or nonessential) relative clauses. A non-restrictive or non-essential clause is one that could be dropped without changing the basic meaning of the sentence. It differs from a restrictive clause, which can't be dropped without changing the basic meaning. (In the examples below, the clauses are in bold.)

> **Restrictive:** Jim, **who didn't understand what I was talking about**, nodded.

> **Non-Restrictive:** Mae looked blankly at the book **that her grandmother gave her.**

Sometimes the comma makes all the difference in the meaning.

> **Restrictive:** The puppy bounded over to the first boy **who smiled at him.**

> **Non-Restrictive:** The puppy bounded over to the first boy, **who smiled at him**.

2.6 To set off NON-restrictive phrases. Non-restrictive phrases are set off by commas, just as nonrestrictive clauses are. Restrictive phrases are not.

> **Restrictive:** The man **in the brown coat** started to walk away.

> **Non-Restrictive:** The white horse, **in a state of panic**, broke out of the corral.

PRACTICE

Punctuate these sentences correctly by adding commas where needed.

6   Gwen who used to be my best friend doesn't want to be with me any more.

7   I don't like anyone who won't tell me the truth.

8   Darkwood Forest a place of mystery sheltered a band of outlaws who called themselves "Raven Hood and his Easily Irritated Men."

9   Vince's attorney smiling gently pointed out that Vince was five thousand miles away at the time the crime was committed.

The comma rules on this page deal with some **more items that are set off** by commas. **Use commas—**

2.7   To set off certain sentence interrupters. Expressions like of course or naturally, which interrupt a sentence, are usually set off by commas.

> Edna, **of course**, was nowhere to be found.

2.8   To set off the parts of dates and addresses.

> Manfred moved to Paris, **France**, on July 13, **1789**, just in time for the French Revolution.

2.9   To set off nouns of address. When a person is spoken to by his or her name or title, that name or title is set off by commas.

> Please, **Your Honor**, I can explain.
>
> Tell me, **Ned**, are you coming or not?
>
> Yes, **Dad**, I've finished my homework.

Two special comma rules involve letter writing. Place a comma—

2.10   After the "Dear—" in a friendly letter. (In a business letter, you use a colon, as discussed later.)

> Dear Ted,   Dear Lucy,   Dear Mom,

2.11   After words like "Yours sincerely," at the end of a letter.

> Very truly yours,   Love,   Sincerely,

PRACTICE

Punctuate these sentences correctly by adding commas where needed.

10   The computer as a result was totally destroyed.

11   Tell me Sue-Ellen do you really think that dress looks good on you?

12   On July 4 1776 Congress approved the Declaration of Independence but the actual signing took place in August.

13   *Dear Henry*

   Don't even think of showing your face around here again.

   Best regards

   Frank

The comma rules on this page deal with introductory commas, that is, after words, phrases, and clauses at the beginning of a sentence. Place a comma—

2.13 After certain introductory words and phrases that don't have a strong connection to the rest of the sentence.

   Naturally, Ross came in first.   Sure, you always blame me.

2.14 After two or more introductory prepositional phrases.

   In the middle of the night, we heard Martin stumbling down the stairs.

   Long before the start of the race to Dutton, I predicted June would win.

After a single prepositional phrase at the beginning of a sentence, you don't usually need a comma. However, you can put one in if the phrase is a long one.

2.15 After an introductory dependent clause. Clauses that begin with the words *if*, *after*, before, when, because, and other subordinating conjunctions are followed by a comma when they begin a sentence.

   When Justin turned around, the dark shape vanished behind the trees.

   Although Cecile voted for the Amazon jungles, the family decided to go to Disneyland.

2.16 After introductory items, when the reader might be confused if there was no comma.

   In writing, your letters should be easy to read.

> The use of commas in punctuating quotations is explained in Section 7.

PRACTICE

Punctuate these sentences correctly by adding commas where needed.

14   Without a traffic light at the corner of Fourth and Main accidents will continue to happen regularly.

15   Before Marie could get to her car the rain came pouring down.

16   If we don't get rain soon the crops may die.

17   Soon after the store was closed for good. (Hint: This tests Rule 2.16.)

18   Anyway we'll probably go right home after the movie.

3. Semicolons

A semicolon usually indicates a stronger break in the flow of a sentence than a comma does.
Use a semicolon—

3.1   Between independent clauses that are *not* joined by a conjunction.

> Luis preferred the pizza; Bonnie went for the tacos.

A semicolon often is used to cure the error called a *run-on*, that is, two independent clauses (or sentences) run together without conjunction or punctuation.

> **Run-On:**   Annie tried to help Dwayne just got in the way.

> **Semicolon Cure:**   Annie tried to help; Dwayne just got in the way.

3.2   Between clauses connected by a word like however. The following words are often used to connect clauses:

however	*nevertheless*	*therefore*	*thus*	*moreover*
besides	*hence*	*accordingly*	*still*	*otherwise*

Whenever the second clause begins with one of these words—a semicolon goes before it, and a comma goes after it.

> Nelson announced that he intended to sail around the world; **however**, he had neglected to acquire a boat.

PRACTICE

These sentences test you on both commas and semicolons. Punctuate these sentences correctly by adding the appropriate punctuation marks where needed.

1   Neatness Veronica may not be the sign of an orderly mind however I still suggest you clean out your locker.

2   I ordered a burger fries and onion rings Melinda took one look at the menu and walked out.

3   It had been raining for seven hours and the field was flooded an inch deep with muddy water nevertheless Jeanette insisted that there was no reason to put off starting the game.

4   I broke my collar bone and Stuart broke his leg still the ski trip wasn't a total loss.

4. Colons

A colon is one punctuation mark that is not used very often. In formal writing it usually introduces something. **Use a colon—**

4.1   **In formal writing, to introduce a list of things**. For an example, look at Semicolon Rule 3.2. It is also used in place of expressions like *for instance or for example*.

> The expedition leaders brought lots of useful items: food and water, warm clothing, direction finders and maps, all-terrain vehicles, *Stearns' Emergency Truck Repair Manual*, and much more.

4.2   **After the "Dear —" in a business letter.** (In a friendly letter, you use a comma, as discussed earlier.)

> Dear Sir: Dear Mr. President: To whom it may concern:

4.3   **In writing the time of day, between the hour and the minute.**

> At exactly **5:35** Alexander showed up—two hours late, as usual.

5. Dashes

A dash usually shows a break in thought. It is often used in informal writing. Use a dash—

5.1   **To mark a sudden change in the direction of a sentence.**

> Every time I try to finish, you just—oh, never mind.

> I walked over to Marnie, smiled, and—well, I couldn't seem to get a word out.

5.2 **To set off something more strongly than commas do.** Remember to use two dashes to set off an item, not a dash and a comma.

> Carlos—he's the kid who's always hanging around with Paulie—got into a bad argument with the teacher this morning.

> The question—and it's a hard one—is whether to move in April or May.

PRACTICE

Punctuate these sentences correctly by adding a colon or a dash wherever they are needed.

1   I've never known the 330 bus to get here before 345.

2   The teacher gathered all her materials for administering the examination pens, paper, a watch for timing, and a copy of the test.

3   Dear Senator Lang

6. Parentheses

Parentheses are used to enclose material that does not have a close connection with the material around it. **Place parentheses—**

6.1 **Around material that has little or no grammatical connection with the rest of the sentence.**

> My email address (I just got online last week) is wcoyote@roadrunner.net.

6.2 **Around definitions and explanations.** In this use—which is optional—the parentheses replace dashes or commas. This use is particularly common in technical writing or when a technical term is being explained.

> Annelids **(segmented worms)** are more closely related to arthropods **(insects, spiders, crabs, etc.)** than you might think from looking at them.

6.3 **You should always use both parentheses.** Sometimes people forget and leave out the second one. Don't make this mistake!

> **Wrong:**   Jughead (it was his brother's name for him walked into the room.

> **Correct:**   Jughead (it was his brother's name for him) walked into the room.

6.4 **Punctuating a sentence inside parentheses.** Sometimes parentheses enclose a complete sentence. If this is inside another sentence, its first word is *not* capitalized, and its period is omitted.

> My sister Rose **(she's the one you thought was so funny)** is coming home next week.

> Otherwise, punctuate in the usual way.

> My sister Rose is coming home next week. **(She's the one you thought was so funny.)**

PRACTICE

Punctuate these sentences correctly by adding parentheses—and whatever additional punctuation and capital letters are needed.

1   Press the CANCEL button it's the one shaped like an arrow to end the program.

2   A lahar a mudflow of volcanic ash and water flowed down the volcano, buried the town, and then hardened like cement.

3   Shut off the display it will shut off automatically in ten minutes if you forget this step and then close down the printer.

7. Apostrophes

An apostrophe is a punctuation mark that appears as part of a word. Its main uses are to form possessives and to indicate missing letters in contractions. **Use an apostrophe—**

7.1   To form the possessives of nouns and indefinite pronouns.

- for singular nouns and *indefinite* pronouns, add **'s**.

    a dog's life   Bill's nose   Mrs. Jackson's class
    everyone's opinion

- for plural nouns ending in -s, just add an apostrophe alone.

    The dogs' tails   the Harrisons' house

- for plural nouns that *don't* end in –s, add **'s** (just like a singular noun).

    the people**'s** rights   the children**'s** shouts

7.2   In contractions. Put the apostrophe in place of the letters that are dropped.

    isn't   can't   won't   couldn't   don't   hasn't   weren't

7.3   Common mistakes with apostrophes. Don't make them!

- Don't confuse the words *its* and *it's*.

    It's is a contraction of it is. It has an apostrophe.

    Its is a possessive. It does *not* have an apostrophe.

    Scientists have found that **it's** not possible for a cat to lick **its** own neck

- In a contraction, do *not* put the apostrophe between the two words. Put it in place of the missing letter or letters.

    Wrong: do'nt   is'nt   did'nt

    Correct: don't   isn't   didn't

PRACTICE

Punctuate these sentences correctly by adding apostrophes where needed.

1   Its a lovely day today.

2   I wont be needing anyones help on this project.

3   Selenas car was missing its rear license plate.

4   The peoples rights cant be taken away by a politicians order.

5   Dont forget to put the workers tools someplace away from the babys hands.

8. Punctuating Quotations

When you punctuate a direct quotation—a person's exact words or the exact words of a piece of writing—you must pay attention to capitalization as well as to commas and periods and the placement of quotation marks. Follow these rules.

8.1   Place the speakers' exact words in quotation marks.

> "**Hurry up,**" said Louis. "**The movie starts in fifteen minutes.**"
> Amy answered, "**Why? I'm not in any hurry.**"

8.2   The quoted words begin with a capital letter.

> "**H**urry up," said Louis. "**T**he movie starts in fifteen minutes."
> Amy answered, "**W**hy? I'm not in any hurry."
> "**W**ell," her brother responded, "it takes twenty minutes to walk to the theater."

In the third sentence above, notice that the quoted sentence is broken into two parts by the words her brother responded. The continuation starts with a small letter because it's not really a new sentence.

> "Well," her brother responded, "**i**t takes twenty minutes to walk to the theater."

8.3   A comma separates words like *he said* and *she answered* from the quoted words.

> "Hurry up," said Louis. "The movie starts in fifteen minutes."
> Amy answered, "Why? I'm not in any hurry."
> "Well," her brother responded, "it takes twenty minutes to walk to the theater."

Notice that commas and periods always go **before** the quotation marks.

> **Wrong:**   "Hurry up**",** said Louis. "The movie starts in fifteen minutes**".**
>
> **Correct**:   "Hurry up**,**" said Louis. "The movie starts in fifteen minutes**.**"

9. Capitalization

9.1 Capitalize the first word of a sentence.

My bicycle once belonged to my grandfather.

9.2 Capitalize the pronoun *I*. (Not all languages do this. For example, Spanish and French don't.)

Everyone wonders if **I** am being serious when **I** say that **I** want to be an explorer.

9.3 Capitalize Proper Nouns. A proper noun is the name of a particular person, place, or thing.

Names:	Lisa Jones	Peter Chang
	Andrew McNeill	Luella C. Carver

Places:	Gulf of Mexico	China
	Louisiana	Baton Rouge
	United States of America	Yellowstone National Park
		Caddo County the South

Things:	the Constitution	the Senate
	the Washington Monument	Microsoft Corp.

Notice that you capitalize all parts of a place name like Yellowstone National Park or of a company like Microsoft Corporation.

8.4 Capitalize people's titles before their names.

Dr. Rucker	Admiral Grommet	Father Breaux
Mr. Lee	Ms. Heath	Mrs. Lopez

8.5 Capitalize names of nationalities and languages.

French	German	Japanese	English
Cherokee	Navajo	Hmong	

8.6 Capitalize the names of days of the week and months of the year.

Wednesday   Saturday   September   April

But do *not* capitalize the names of seasons.

summer   fall   winter   spring   autumn

8.7 Capitalize the names of holidays.

Christmas   Fourth of July   Independence Day   Thanksgiving

PRACTICE

Rewrite each sentence, inserting capitals as necessary.

1   my family and I will be back on tuesday, september 6, after labor day.

_____

_____

2   i heard mrs. peterson learned chinese and went to beijing, china, last fall.

_____

_____

8.8   Capitalize the words in the salutation of a letter. The salutation is the part at the beginning that usually begins "Dear —."

> **Dear Aunt Mary,   Dear Sir: Dear Mr. President:**

8.9   Capitalize the first word of the closing of a letter. (Don't capitalize the words after the first one.)

> **Sincerely yours,   Very truly yours,   Love,**

The capitalization and punctuation of **titles** can get a little complicated. Here are the rules:

8.10 Capitalize the titles of books, songs, stories, plays, movies, and the like. This rule is actually a little more complicate than the simple statement. Here are the details:

> a) Always capitalize the **first** and **last** words of the title.
>
> b) Otherwise, do *not* capitalize these kinds of words:
>
>   **coordinating conjunctions: and, but, or, nor, for, yet**
>   **short prepositions** (four words or less): **in, on, of, into, to, at,** etc.
>   **articles: a, an,** and **the**

The titles of long works like books, movies, plays, and television series go in italics (if printed) or are underlined. Titles of short works like stories, poems, and songs are set off by quotation marks.

> "**The Star-Spangled Banner**"
> *The Wizard of Oz* (or <u>The Wizard of Oz</u>)
> *Gone with the Wind* (or <u>Gone with the Wind</u>)
> "**America the Beautiful**"
> *Gilligan's Island* (or <u>Gilligan's Island</u>)
> "**The Last Leaf**" (a short story)

Usage

1. Pronouns

Pronouns are words like *I, me, mine, we, you, he, she, it,* and similar words that stand for or replace nouns. Pronouns have different forms. To choose the correct form, you need to look at how the pronoun is used in the sentence.

1.1   When a pronoun is the subject of a sentence, it takes one of these forms:

> *I   you   he   she   it   we   they*

She likes parrots.
You are mistaken.
Every evening **they** watch TV for two hours.

1.2   Even when there are two or more subjects, the subject pronouns must still be in the subject form.

> **Wrong:**   **Nancy and me** went to the movies.
>
> **Wrong:**   **Me and Nancy** went to the movies.
>
> **Correct:**   **Nancy and I** went to the movies.

"Me and Nancy" might sound all right at first. But you can hear it's wrong if you say it with just the pronoun: "Me went to the movies."

1.3   After a verb or a preposition (words like to, of, for between, etc.) pronouns have what is called the object form:

> *me   you   him   her   it   us   them*

Talk to **me**.
I see **you**.
It's easy for **her**. Nobody noticed **them**.

1.4   When there are two or more objects, all object pronouns must still be in the object form.

> **Wrong:**   The gorilla cautiously approached **Fred and I**.
>
> **Correct:**   The gorilla cautiously approached **Fred and me**.

"Fred and I" might sound all right at first. But you can hear it's wrong if you say it with just the pronoun: "The gorilla cautiously approached I."

PRACTICE

Rewrite each sentence, correcting any mistakes in usage.

1   Sue and me didn't agree on how to handle the issues between her and Max.

_____

_____

2   Between you and I, they are both just being stubborn.

_____

_____

1.5   To show possession, the following adjective forms of pronouns are used:

| **Before Nouns:** | *my* | *your* | *his* | *her* | *its* | *our* | *their* |

| **By Themselves:** | *mine* | *yours* | *his* | *hers* | *its* | *ours* | *theirs* |

This is **my** topic.
The topic is **mine**.
Its teeth narrowly missed **her** arm.

There are two tricky things to watch out for:

• The possessives yours, his, hers, its, ours, and theirs are *not* written with apostrophes. (This is unlike noun possessives like dog's, which do take apostrophes.)

• Its (no apostrophe) is a possessive. It's (with an apostrophe) means "it is." This often turns up on tests!

• The possessives of indefinite pronouns *do* have apostrophes:

   everyone's   someone's   enerybody's   somebody's

1.6   A pronoun must agree with its antecedent in number.   That is, if whatever a pronoun refers to (called the *antecedent*) is singular, the pronoun must be singular too. If it's plural, the pronoun must be plural.

Wrong: Our dogs have learned to look out for **themself**.

Correct: Our dogs have learned to look out for **themselves**.

Most confusion comes when another noun comes between the pronoun and its antecedent:

Wrong: The first of these problems will take care of **themselves**.

Correct: The first of these problems will take care of **itself**.

In this example, the pronoun (the last word in the sentence) refers to the noun *first*, not the noun *problems*. Should take the singular form *itself*, not the plural form *themselves*.

PRACTICE

Rewrite each sentence, correcting any mistakes in usage.

3 Marie insisted that the bag with her initials that was found under all her friends' coats wasn't theirs.

_____

_____

4 But its pretty obvious that the bag really was her's.

_____

2. Verbs and Verb Forms

2.2 The tense of a verb must match the sense of the sentence. The form of a verb (called its tense) shows the time that the action of a verb is taking place. (For example. The form *walked* shows past time.) The tense of the verb must match the meaning of the sentence.

> **Wrong:**   Back in Colonial times, most people **make** their own clothes.
>
> **Correct:**   Back in Colonial times, most people **made** their own clothes.

This is very frequently tested on reading and writing tests.

2.3 Use the correct forms of irregular verbs. Most verbs add the ending *–ed* to show past time. But many common ones, called irregular verbs, do not. A list of the most common **irregular verbs** is on the following page.

> **Wrong:**   The balloon **busted** when I **blowed** it up.
>
> **Correct:**   The balloon **burst** when I **blew** it up.

 WARNING: Tests like TAKS often test you on the forms of irregular verbs.

2.3 Don't use the form ain't. Use the correct form of *be* or *have* in its place.

> **Wrong:**   No, we **ain't** gone yet. He **ain't** going, and I **ain't** going either.
>
> **Correct:**   No, we **haven't** gone yet. He **isn't** going, and **I'm not** going either.

IRREGULAR VERB	PAST TENSE	FORM USED WITH HAVE OR BE
become	became	(has) become
begin	began	(has) begun
blow	blew	(has) blown
break	broke	(has) broken
bring	brought	(has) brought
burst	burst	(has) burst
buy	bought	(has) bought
catch	caught	(has) caught
choose	chose	(has) chosen
come	came	(has) come
cut	cut	(has) cut
dive	dove or dived	(has) dived
do	did	(has) done
eat	ate	(has) eaten
fly	flew	(has) flown
forget	forgot	(has)forgotten
hang	hung	(has) hung
get	got	(has) got or gotten
give	gave	(has) given
go	went	(has) gone
grow	grew	(has) grown
have, has	had	(has) has had
hit	hit	(has) hit
hurt	hurt	(has) hurt
know	knew	(has) known
leave	left	(has) left
let	let	(has) let
mean	meant	(has) meant
ride	rode	(has) ridden
ring	rang	(has) rung
run	ran	(has) run
see	saw	(has) seen
shine	shone	(has) shown
sing	sang	(has) sung
spring	sprang or sprung	(has) sprung
strike	struck	(has) struck
swim	swam	(has) swum
take	took	(has) taken
tell	told	(has) told
think	thought	(has) thought
throw	throw	(has) thrown
write	wrote	(has) written

And the special verb **be**:

Am, is, are	was, were	(has) been

1.3 **Don't get tripped up by any of these verb pairs, which are frequently confused.**
Notice that many of them are irregular verbs.

VERB	PAST FORMS		MEANING
lay laid	**(has)**	**laid**	to place something or put it down flat
lie lay	**(has)**	**lain**	to rest or recline (lie down)

I **laid** the book on the chair *but* I **lay** down to sleep.

set set	**(has)**	**set**	to put something down, or to harden like plaster or glue
sit sat	**(has)**	**sat**	to rest on a chair or couch

I **set** the book on the table *but* I **sat** down on the chair.

let let	**(has)**	**let**	to permit (or to rent)
leave left	**(has)**	**left**	to go away or to abandon (to leave something behind)

I **let** him get away *but* I **left** his brother behind.

raise raised	**(has)**	**raised**	to lift something up
rise rose	**(has)**	**risen**	to get up or to move in an upward direction

I **raised** my head *but* I **rose** before dawn.

> **NOTICE:**
> Lie meaning "to tell an untruth" is a regular verb whose past form is lied.

PRACTICE

Rewrite each sentence, correcting any mistakes in usage.

6 Jesse came in, set his cup down, and set down on the edge of the bed.

_____

7 I laid down on the grass on the same spot where I had laid yesterday.

_____

8 For three weeks now the sun has rose after seven o'clock.

_____

9 The principal let me leave, but I left my homework assignment in her office.

_____

10 Lay the map back on the floor just the way it lay when you came in.

_____

3. Subject–Verb Agreement

If the verb of a sentence is in the present tense, the form that it takes depends on whether the subject of the sentence is singular or plural. If the subject is a pronoun, the form the verb takes also depends on what pronoun it is. This is called agreement. We say that a verb must agree with its subject—that is, its form depends on what the subject is.

3.1 **The present tense of a verb ends in** *–s* **or** *–es* **when the subject is a singular noun or one of these pronouns:** *he, she, it.*

> **Bernice plays** piano and violin like a professional.
>
> However, **she sings** like a frog.

3.2 **The present tense of a verb does NOT end in** *–s* **or** *–es* **when the subject is a plural noun or one of these pronouns:** *I, you, we, they.*

> **People say** that **coyotes howl** at the moon.
>
> **They** also **howl** when Bernice sings.

> **NOTICE:**
> The verb *have* has the special form *has* in these situations.

3.3 **A compound subject (two or more subjects) follows the rule for plural subjects.**

> **Exercise** and **weight training help** Dr. Benton stay in shape.

3.4 **The verb** *be* **is special. It has several different forms in both the present tense and the past. Make sure you know all these forms.**

> **Present:**   **I am**
> **he**, **she**, or **it** (or a singular noun) **is**
> **you, we,** or **they** (or a plural noun) **are**
>
> **Past:**   **I, he, she,** or **it** (or a singular noun) **was**
> **you, we,** or **they** (or a plural noun) **were**

PRACTICE

After each sentence write the correct form of the verb or verbs that are shown in parentheses.

1   Rajiv (be, am, is, are) my second cousin. _____

2   Minnie (was, were) working at the store . _____

3   Our team (win, wins) more games than it (lose, loses). _____

4   The point of every one of my jokes (was, were) lost on George. _____

5   Ruth's guitar and Tom's fiddle (am, is, are) both out of tune. _____

4. Adjectives and Adverbs

Adjectives are words that **modify** (describe or tell about) nouns.

> His **long**, **thin** face was **sad**, with **red** eyes and a **droopy** mustache.

Adverbs are words that modify verbs, adjectives, or other adverbs. They often answer questions like *how*, *where*, and *when*.

> **Quickly** the squirrel jumped **away**, **skillfully** avoiding the strikes of an **increasingly** angry snake.

Many adverbs are formed by adding the ending *–ly* to an adjective—but some of the most important do not, and not all words ending in *–ly* are adverbs.

4.1   Don't use an adjective in place of an adverb.

> **Wrong:**   He seems **real** nice.

> **Correct:**   He seems **really** nice.

4.2   Don't confuse the adjective *good* with the adverb *well* (meaning "in a good manner" or with the adjective well (meaning "healthy"). Most problems occur when *good* or *well* comes after the verb. Here are some guidelines:

1)   After the verbs *look*, *feel*, *seem*, *appear* and *be*, the usual word is *good*. The word well after these words usually means "healthy." The verbs *smell*, *taste*, and *sound* are also usually followed by *good*.

> He looks **good**. (I like the way he looks.)
> He looks **well**. (He looks healthy)
> This meat doesn't smell **good** or taste **good** to me.

2)   After most other verbs the most likely word is *well*.

> **Wrong:**   I can't see the stage too **good**.
> **Correct:**   I can't see the stage too **well**.

PRACTICE

Choose the correct word from each set of parentheses and write it after the sentence.

1   I can't think too (good, well) if people are shouting at me. _____

2   Rita felt sick, but the doctor insisted she was (good, well). _____

3   How (good, well) can you read this? _____

4   You have to speak (clear, clearly) when you talk to Mr. McBean. _____

5   I'm (real, really) sorry to hear that. _____

5. Comparatives and Superlatives

The **comparative** form of an adjective or adverb is a form that either has the word more in front of it or that has the ending *–er*.

> You are **more confident** than I am that you are **stronger** than "Crusher" Creel.

The **superlative** form of an adjective or adverb is a form that either has the word most in front of it or that has the ending *–est*.

> Wayne is the **most experienced** skater, but Jeremy is the **fastest**.

5.1 **Don't use the superlative form when comparing only two things. Use the comparative form.**

> **Wrong:**   Jenny is the **oldest** of the two sisters.
>
> **Correct:**   Jenny is the **older** of the two sisters.

5.2 **Don't use a double comparative or a double superlative.** That is, don't put more or most in front of a form ending in *-er* or *–est*.

> **Wrong:**   Your pizza is **more bigger** than mine.
>
> **Correct:**   Your pizza is **bigger** than mine.
>
> **Wrong:**   This is Jim's **most finest** hour.
>
> **Correct:**   This is Jim's **finest** hour.

5.3 **Memorize these irregularly formed comparatives and superlatives.**

	COMPARATIVE	SUPERLATIVE
good	better	best
well	better	best
bad	worse	worst
many or **much**	more	most
far	farther or further	farthest or furthest
little	less	least

PRACTICE

Write the correct form of any comparatives or superlatives in the blank sentence. If the sentence is correct as is, leave the line blank.

1 More better you should apologize than hold a grudge forever. _____

2 Harris and Truman are both good cooks, but of the two, Truman makes the best barbecue. _____

3 This is the baddest-tasting chicken that I have ever eaten. _____

4 That last storm was worser than any we have had this year. _____

5 The most far thing we can see with the naked eye is the Andromeda Galaxy. _____

6. Special Usage Problems

6.1 Do not use double negatives. Negatives are words like the following.

> **No not never nobody no one**
> **nothing hardly scarcely barely**

Don't use more than one negative in a simple sentence or a clause.

> **Wrong**:   Do**n't never** do that again.
>
> **Correct**: **Never** do that again.
>
> **Wrong**:   I ca**n't hardly** stand it.
>
> **Correct**: I can **hardly** stand it.

6.2 Don't use the form *ain't*. Use the correct form of *be* or *have* in its place.

> **Wrong**:   No, we **ain't** gone yet. He **ain't** going, and I **ain't** going either.
>
> **Correct**: No, we **haven't** gone yet. He **isn't** going, and **I'm not** going either.

PRACTICE

Rewrite each sentence, correcting any errors in usage.

1 Nobody ain't never told me nothing like that.

_____

2 Hardly nobody was interested in Nelson's speech.

_____

Sentence Construction

1. Incomplete Sentences (Sentence Fragments)

A sentence fragment, or incomplete sentence, is a group of words that looks like a sentence but isn't one. It begins with a capital and ends with a period—but it is not a complete sentence. Here are two examples:

Fragment: Hanging onto the vine with my teeth.

Fragment: Where the bats were sleeping.

On tests and in your own writing, a sentence fragment is a mistake that needs to be corrected. Here are two common types.

1.1 **Recognize fragments that begin with words like *when, because, before, although, etc.*** Words like these introduce dependent clauses—clauses that have a subject and a verb, but that need to be attached to another sentence.

> We avoided the cave. **Where the bats were sleeping**. Instead, we crawled into a side passage.

1.2 **Recognize fragments that begin with words that end in *-ing* or *–ed*.** These words introduce phrases that are often found as fragments.

> A wicked-looking snake hung down from a branch nearby. **Hanging onto the vine with my teeth**. I reached into my pocket and brought out my knife.

1.3 **Fix a fragment by making it part of the sentence that it belongs with.**

> **We avoided the cave where the bats were sleeping**. Instead, we crawled into a side passage.

> A wicked-looking snake hung down from a branch nearby. **Hanging onto the vine with my teeth, I reached into my pocket and brought out my knife.**

PRACTICE

Rewrite these sentences, fixing any fragments.

1   Tracy's eyes narrowed. When she saw Linda's smile. It wasn't a nice smile.

_____

2   If I had one wish. It would be for a car. I'd like a driver's license, too.

_____

3   I heard a shout. Then I saw a man. Running away from the store.

_____

2. Run-on Sentences

A run-on sentence is two or more sentences that are joined together incorrectly.

2.1 **Recognize the two most common kinds of run-ons.** One common kind of run-on consists of two sentences run together with no punctuation or coordinating conjunction (a connecting word like and, or, so, or but).

> The distant howling grew closer nobody spoke or moved.

The second kind of run-on joins together sentences with a comma alone but no connecting word.

> The distant howling grew closer, nobody spoke or moved.

There are several ways to correct a run-on. Four of the most-frequently used ones are listed below.

2.2 **Correct a run-on with a comma and a coordinating conjunction.**
Look back at Punctuation Rule 2.3.

> The distant howling grew closer, **but** nobody spoke or moved.

2.3 **Correct a run-on with a semicolon.** Look back at Punctuation Rule 3.1. You may want to add a transition word to smooth over the junction between the two parts of the sentence.

> The distant howling grew closer; **still**, nobody spoke or moved.

2.4 **Correct a run-on by breaking it into two sentences.**

> The distant howling grew closer. **N**obody spoke or moved.

2.5 **Correct a run-on by turning one of the sentences into a dependent clause.** There are many ways to do this, depending on the meaning the writer wishes to convey. Look back at Punctuation Rule 2.15.

> **Although** the distant howling grew closer, nobody spoke or moved.

PRACTICE

On a separate sheet of paper, correct the following run-ons. Use a different method for each one.

1   The water rushed over the falls Sally pulled her canoe to the shore.

2   Truman stared down in horror, under the carpet something was moving.

3   My real first name is Othniel, I think the name is as stupid as you probably do.

4   I broke my leg I couldn't be in the relay race.

Spelling

There are two ways for you to brush up on your spelling. One is to learn—and apply—some of the important spelling rules. The other is to memorize lists of words that people frequently misspell.

1. Spelling Rules

1.1 **IE or EI?** There's a famous spelling rhyme that you should memorize:

Put *i* before *e*	**Examples:**	bel**ie**ve gr**ie**f
Except after *c*,	**Examples:**	conc**ei**ve dec**ei**t
Or when sounded long **a**		
as in n**ei**ghbor and w**ei**gh.		

There are several exceptions to the rule. The following two sentences contain the main ones. Unfortunately, they don't make a great deal of sense, but they do the job.

I Before E:	N**ei**ther l**ei**sured for**ei**gn sh**ei**k s**ei**zed the w**ei**rd h**ei**ght as forf**ei**t for their h**ei**fers' prot**ei**n.
Except After C:	A financ**ie**r is a spec**ie**s of sc**ie**ntist.

1.2 **The sound of *k*.** At the beginning of a word, the sound of *k* is usually spelled with a *c*—unless it is followed by *e* or *i*. Before *e* or *i*, the *k*-sound is usually spelled with a *k*.

Usually:	**c**ase	**c**an	**c**old	**c**ube	**c**areer
Before *E* or *I*:	**k**ettle	**k**een	**k**iss	**k**indle	
Exceptions:	**k**arate	**k**angaroo	**k**oala	**k**ayak	

1.3 **Prefixes.** This is the easiest rule of all. When a prefix is added to a word, there is no spelling change at all.

re + place = replace   mis + place = misplace   co + operate = cooperate

PRACTICE

On the line after each sentence, rewrite any wrongly spelled words correctly.

1   Peicing together the meaning of a batch of mispelled words is a science. _____

2   After a long riegn, the cheif received the thanks of his people. _____

3   It's a releif to know that the cieling is not going to collapse. _____

4   Martin feigned ignorance of the rules as he siezed the ball and ran with it. _____

The spelling rules on this page deal with spelling changes at the end of a word when you add a suffix to it.

1.4 **Keeping or dropping a final –e.** Drop the final –e of a word when you add a suffix beginning with a **vowel**. Keep it when you add a suffix beginning with a **consonant**.

> **Drop the –E:** place + –ing = **placing** like + –able = **likable**

> **Keep the –E:** place + –**m**ent = placement (suffix begins with a consonant)

Keep the –e if the suffix begins with an a or an o. You need the -e to preserve the s-sound of the letter c or the j-sound of then letter g.

> pea**c**e + -**a**ble = peac**e**able   mana**g**e + -**a**ble = manag**e**able

Memorize these three exceptions. They often appear on tests!

> judgment   acknowledgment   argument

1.5 **Changing final –y to –i.** Make the change if there is a **consonant** before the –y and if the suffix does *not* already begin with i.

> **Drop the –Y:** happ**y** + –est = happ**i**est tr**y** + –**es** = tr**i**es

> **Keep the –Y:** to**y** + –**s** = toys   sa**y** + –**s** = says (no vowel before the –y)

> **Keep the –Y:** tr**y** + –ing = tr**y**ing den**y** + –ing = den**y**ing (suffix beginswith –i)

1.6 **Doubling a final consonant before a suffix beginning with a vowel.** Make the change if the word ends with the letter combination **CVC** (consonant-vowel-consonant) and if—

- the base word has only one syllable or is accented on the last syllable.

> **Double the Consonant:** d**rop** + –ing = dro**pp**ing (CVC; one syllable)

> **Double the Consonant:** be**gin** + –er = begi**nn**er (CVC; accent on last syllable)

> **Do Not Double the Consonant:** shake + –er = shaker (not CVC)

> **Do Not Double the Consonant:** tra**vel** + –ing (accent not on last syllable)

PRACTICE

If an underlined word is misspelled, cross it out and write the correct spelling above it.

5   Cinderella was <u>hopful</u> that her <u>engagement</u> to the prince would be <u>enjoiable</u>.

6   In my <u>judgement</u>, the <u>arguement</u> about who is <u>stronggest</u> is <u>tiresome</u>.

7   Sandra has not yet <u>tryed</u> to see if there is any way of <u>controling</u> her temper.

8   It <u>occured</u> to me that Bernice has recently <u>shuned</u> going <u>shoping</u> with me.

The spelling rules on this page deal with spelling changes in forming the plurals of nouns.

1.7 **Adding –s or –es.** The usual way of forming the plural of a noun is to add an –s. However, you add –es to most nouns ending in –s, –z, –sh, –ch, or –x. (Notice that these words all end with a hissing or buzzing sound.) You may have to follow Spelling Rule 1.6 when you add –es.

> **Add –S:** dog**s**   cat**s**   bicycle**s**   computer**s**   eagle**s**   lamp**s**

> **Add –ES:** glass**es**   eyelash**es**   porch**es**   fox**es**

1.8 **Nouns ending in –y.** Form the plural in the usual way, by adding an –s, if there is a **vowel** before the –y. But if the letter before the –y is a **consonant**, change the –y to –i and add –es.

> **Add –S:** boy, boy**s**   day, day**s**   mon**k**ey, mon**k**ey**s** (vowel before the –y)

> **Add –ES:** ba**b**y, ba**b**i**es**   **fl**y, **fl**i**es**   (consonant before the –y)

1.9 **Nouns ending in –o.** These are like nouns ending in –y. Form the plural in the usual way, by adding an –s, if there is a **vowel** before the –o. But add –es if the letter before the –o is a **consonant**.

> **Add –S:** ratio, ratio**s**   rod**e**o, rod**e**o**s** (vowel before the –o)

> **Add –ES:** volca**n**o, volca**n**o**es**   he**r**o, he**r**o**es** (consonant before the –o)

> **Exceptions:** solo**s**, soprano**s**, and other Italian words about music

1.10 **Nouns ending in –f and –fe.** The pronunciation gives the clue. If the plural is pronounced –fs, spell it that way. If it's pronounced –vz, spell it –ves.

> **Add –S:** roof, roof**s**   chief, chief**s**

> **Spelled –VES:** elf, el**ves**   knife, kni**ves**

PRACTICE

After each of the following words, write its plural.

9 leaf _____   16 loaf _____   23 mango _____

10 echo _____   17 patio _____   24 video _____

11 donkey _____   18 toy _____   25 box _____

12 dish _____   19 belief _____   26 key _____

13 cliff _____   20 space _____

14 latch _____   21 potato _____

15 cry _____   22 cello _____

2. Spelling Lists

The English language is famous for its truly awful spelling system. One well-known writer suggested that the imaginary word *ghoti* could be pronounced "fish": pronounce the *gh* as in *rough*, the *o* as in *women*, and the *ti* as in *nation*. With a spelling system like this, you have to memorize the spellings of lots of words.

Beginning on the next page are lists of words that students at your grade level often misspell. Some may look really easy to you, but all have caused trouble to someone.

There are three sets of lists:

1. Words that are frequently confused.
2. Words that are misspelled because they were not spelled according to the rules in the previous section.
3. Other frequently misspelled words.

There are more than 500 words on all these lists, which is a lot. To make things easier for you, they have been divided into 25 smaller lists of about 20 words each.

Here's the easiest way to study these words:

- Begin with List 1. Have someone read the words to you. Write each one down.

- Check your words. Mark the ones you spelled wrong. Also mark the words you weren't completely sure of, even if you got them right. You may want someone else to check your list, too, to catch any misspellings you may have missed.

- Study these words until you are sure you know how to spell them. Add them to List 2.

- Keep a separate record of these words, and review them from time to time. They are problem words for you. Continue until you have studied all the lists. If you work on one list a day, you'll master all the words in less than a month.

2.1 Frequently Confused Words

it's ("it is")
its ("belonging to it")
their ("belonging to them")
there ("in that place")
they're (they are)
your
you're
loose
lose

who's ("who is")
whose ("belonging to whom")
passed ("went beyond" or
          ("succeeded on a test")
past (opposite of future)
peace (opposite of war)
piece (a part of something)
too ("also')
to ("toward")
two (2)

2.2   Problems with Spelling Rules

Punctuation Rule 7.1—possessives

everyone's

Punctuation Rule 7.2—contractions

aren't	haven't	that's	we're
couldn't	here's	there's	weren't
didn't	let's	(there is)	what's
doesn't	ma'am	we'll	won't
			wouldn't

Spelling Rule 1.1—ie or ei

fierce	neither
friend	weigh
neighbor	weird
neighborhood	

Spelling Rule 1.4—keeping or dropping final –e

famous	losing	surely
giggling	loving	shining
having	making	

Spelling Rule 1.5—changing or not changing –y to –i

happily	plays	tries
luckily	said	toys
played	says	studying

Spelling Rule 1.6—doubling or not doubling final consonant

expelled	popped	stopped
finally	popping	traveling
getting	referral	tripped
hugged	slammed	swimming
jammed	stepped	tapped

2.3 Other Frequently Misspelled Words

List 1	List 3	List 5	List 7
a lot	basketball	country	everyday
about	because	course	(meaning
absent	been	cousin	"ordinary")
accepted	before	cupboard	everything
accident	believe	daddy	everywhere
address	birthday	dairy	excellent
advise	blackboard	daydreaming	except
afterwards	blonde	dear	excitement
again	blue	decorate	excuse
against	bought	delicious	expect
airplane	bracelet	detention	explain
all right	brakes	diamond	extremely
allowed	burst	dictionary	fainted
along	busy	different	fault
already	buy	dinosaur	favorite
although	buzzer	disappointed	February
always	bye	disaster	feelings
ambulance	California	discipline	first
among	cannot	disturb	football
ankle	celebrate	doctor	forty

List 2	List 4	List 6	List 8
announced	chalkboard	does	forward
announcer	challenge	downstairs	fought
annoyed	championship	dumb	fourth
anymore	charcoal	each other	Friday
anyway	children	early	frightened
apologize	chocolate	earrings	fuel
April	choose	Easter	goes
arithmetic	Christmas	easy	going to
assigned	classmate	elementary	goof-off
assignment	classroom	embarrassed	grade
attack	close	enough	grandparents
attention	clothes	entrance	guard
aunt	color	especially	guess
automobile	come	essay	guitar
awful	commotion	every	half
awhile	competition	every day	halfway
background	concentrate	every time	Halloween
backyard	cookout	everybody	hallway
balloon	cough	everybody	hamburger
barbecue	could		handkerchief

List 9	List 11	List 13	List 15
happened	letter	paddle	safety
hear	library	paid	said
heard	lifeguard	party	sandwiches
height	listening	passed	Santa Claus
hello	little	passenger	Saturday
helmet	lonely	peace	says
here	lying	people	scary
herself	magic	piece	school
himself	many	playground	scissors
hollered	maybe	please	searched
hospital	meant	poison	seat belt
hot dog	meanwhile	potato	secretary
hour	medal	practice	sentence
house	might	pretty	several
hurting	minute	principal	shallow
ice cream	month	probably	shiny
ice-skate	moral	punishment	shoes
ice-skating	morning		since
ignore	mother		sincerely
immediately			

List 10	List 12	List 14	List 16
in trouble	motorcycle	quarter	skiing
incident	movies	quiet	skis
information	myself	quit	soccer
injuries	name	quite	some
instance	nearby	raise	something
instant	necklace	read	sometime
instead	nervous	realize	somewhere
interested	nice	receive	soon
interrupted	no one	received	sore
jealous	none	referee	sprained
jewelry	nonsense	relatives	startled
jewels	nowhere	remember	steal
keyboard	o'clock	right	steering
kickball	off	rooting	stereo
knew	often	rough	stole
know	Olympics	route	store
laid	once	routine	straight
latter	outside	rowdy	substitute
laughter			
lessons			

List 17	List 18	List 19	List 20
summer	throughout	upon	white
Sunday	throws	upstairs	whoever
suppose	tired	used	whole
sure	together	usual	whose
surprise	tomorrow	usually	windshield
surrounded	tonight	vacation	women
suspension	too ("also")	valuable	would
teacher	tournament	very	wrapped
teammates	train	volleyball	wreck
tear	trouble	wear	write
terrible	troublemaker	weather	writing
thank you	truly	Wednesday	wrote
Thanksgiving	Tuesday	were	yeah
themselves	uncomfortable	whatever	you
therefore	unconscious	when	your
they	unfortunately	whenever	("belonging to you")
though	until	where	yourself
thought	unusual	whether	opposite
threw		which	ruined
through		whistle	sugar

Practice Tests

This part of your *Coach* book contains two full-length practice tests, each similar to the actual state test.

- Practice Test 1 contains some tips and hints to guide you

- When you take the second test, you are on your own

Good Luck—and good luck on the real test!

How to Approach the TAKS Test

As you know, the TAKS Language Arts test is based on a triplet—two reading selections and a visual representation that share a topic or a theme. The test makers choose selections that reflect different aspects of the chosen topic. And they even tell you what these important aspects are by asking questions about them. The essay that you will write is based on the same theme.

How can you make use of this knowledge? A successful test-taker will use a procedure something like the one below:

1 Read the writing assignment on page 229 before you do anything else. Ask yourself: What is the topic—the big idea?

Write your answer on the line that follows.

_____

Note that the topic does not refer to your experience only. The phrase "an important part of life" tells you that the topic is *universal*, something that everyone can experience.

2 Next, take a look at the first selection, "Shining Moon." Skim it so that you know in general what it is about. Don't take more than a minute to do this. By reading quickly down the page you can identify the main characters. By reading the headnote (the note at the top) you learn that this is a very old story. Old stories stay in the world's literature because they reflect all human experience—the universal topic that we mentioned above.

3 Glance over the questions that follow the selection. Don't worry about the answer choices—just look at the questions. Focus on the questions that ask something about Aigiarn. Even without answering them, you can form an impression of his character. Do you think Aigiarn is adventurous? Gentle? Passive?

Write your impression on the lines that follow.

_____

_____

_____

_____

4   Now look at the second selection, "Title IX." As you did with "Shining Moon," skim it so that you know what it's about and what the issues involved are. Then skim the questions to see what the important points are.

Write some of those points on the lines below.

_____

_____

_____

_____

5   Go to questions number 29 and 30. These are questions that deal with both selections. Without even reading all the material, you can probably make a good guess at some of the issues involved.

Write your guess here.

_____

_____

_____

_____

6   Finally, take a look at the open-ended questions (numbers 33-35). Of course, you can't answer them now, but you should keep them in mind when you read the selections. They will help you focus your reading.

7   Read the selections, making marks in the margin about points you may want to use in your essay, as well as places where you can find the answers to the questions.

8   Use the information in the graphics to help you get a picture about what else could be happening in a selection.

9   Don't spend more than five minutes on these tasks! Make every second count, though, because when you are finished you will have a good idea about how to answer the questions and write the composition.

Writing Your Composition

Notice that the prompt asks you to write a composition about a universal idea or experience—creating or taking advantages—that appears as a theme in the reading selections and that probably applies to experiences in your own life or the life of someone you know. You should be prepared to use incidents and details from both the selections and your own experiences as sources for support and elaboration in your composition.

The test does not require you to do this. But your composition will probably have more focus and more interest, and will probably receive a higher score if you include both than if you restrict yourself to a very abstract discussion of the topic of the prompt.

When you are citing examples from two sources—the selections and your own experience—you may wish to write a first paragraph that focuses on explaining the idea as it applies generally rather than by plunging directly into an example from your own experience. You can then use examples from the selections and from your general knowledge to give your reader the sense that the issue you are discussing has a broad application. Once you have established the universal aspect of the idea, your own experiences can be used in support of the theme.

Practice Test 1

DIRECTIONS

Read the two selections and the viewing and representing piece. Then answer the questions that follow.

Shining Moon: A Retelling

A retelling by Jessica Wade

The original of this tale is more than 700 years old, and Princess Shining Moon was a real person, famous both for her beauty and her strength. We know her story from the writings of Marco Polo, a famous traveler, who lived at the same time as Shining Moon and heard stories about her when he lived at the court of her great-uncle, the Emperor of China.

1   My name, Aigiarn, means "Shining Moon." I was named after the bright moon that shone on the night of my birth. My mother says that my father Kaidu looked up and said, "That moon is like the woman our daughter will one day become. She will be elegant and beautiful, a source of calm and solace for all of our people."

2   My father is a wise man, but on this occasion, he was decidedly wrong.

3   I am a princess of the Mongols. We are a warring people, led from the arid, treeless steppes of Mongolia to more fertile lands by Chinggis Khan, my great-great-grandfather. We have spread and conquered wherever we go, and we now rule from the Chinese Ocean westward for many thousands of miles to the distant lands where the strange Christian people live.

4   Unlike my great-uncle the Emperor of China, who has grown soft by adopting the habits of those he defeated, my family has not forgotten our traditional ways. We still keep and ride the sturdy horses whose agility and strength allowed our success in battle. We do not bind the feet of our women like the Chinese, or tie ourselves to the land with farms and houses. We live in gers, round tents hung with rich tapestry and always filled with the smoke of burning fire and the sound of talk and laughter.

5   I grew up in a ger, listening with rapt attention to the stories the soldiers and my father shared. They would tell of the

great hunt, the month-long expedition involving the whole army and thousands of horses, or of tremendous battles and joyous victories. I especially loved the secret history, the story of Chinggis Khan's life and how he had led our people to greatness. The men were amused by my eagerness, and they let me accompany them hunting, allowing me to see first-hand the events from their stories. I learned to hunt and track with the best of the men. I could shoot a moving rabbit with my bow and arrow from across a river, and turn backwards in my saddle to do it if I had to. The other girls thought me strange for hunting, and so my friends were mainly the sons of my father's soldiers. Together we wrestled and fought, rode and ran, and learned to make bows and arrows. I simply had no interest in the weaving and cooking that my mother and sisters spent their time on.

6   It soon became clear that I could do more than keep up with the boys—I could surpass them. I grew as tall as my mother by my eleventh birthday, and as tall as my father by my sixteenth. I rode into battle with my father, and I joined in the great hunt, where we rode and slept on horseback for more than 30 days. I was dirty and tired by the end of it, but the bonds I had formed with the other soldiers were unbreakable. The thrill of battle and the exhilaration of the hunt were what I lived for.

7   On my eighteenth birthday, as I knew he would, my father told me I had to marry. It is Mongol tradition that you must marry outside your tribe, and therefore marriage is regarded as a way to build alliances and develop partners in trade. The marriage of a princess could be vital to assuring the wealth and security of her tribe. I understood all this, yet I did not want to marry. As a wife, I could not continue to hunt and fight. I knew the soldiers well, and they would tease a husband whose wife did not stay at home without mercy. I proposed a plan to my father, which, though it would not guarantee I would love my husband, would at least make sure I could respect him.

8   "I will marry," I said. "But first, any suitor must pass a test. He must compete against me in a contest of physical power. It can be hunting, or swimming, anything he likes, but I will not marry him unless he wins. And if he loses, he must pay me a penalty of 100 horses."

9   My father was silent for a moment, but then a small smile

spread across his face. "Aigiarn, you are a shrewd girl," he said, "and at any rate, I would not have you marry a man who was not at least your equal. It will be as you have asked."

10   My father let my plan be known, and soon young men from all the neighboring tribes began to arrive. The first, Tartu, was no match for me. I had met him on the great hunt, and I knew I could best him at any skill. He asked for an hour-long hunt—whoever had trapped the most rabbits at the end of the hour would be declared the winner. He caught seven rabbits; I caught fifteen. Sourly, he gave over his hundred horses.

11   The second man was more inventive. We would run four miles, then swim across a large lake, and then engage in an archery contest. I think he thought his strength as a man could carry him through the running and the swimming, but that mine would be drained, forcing me to miss my marks in the archery. He did best me on the run, but I have always moved well in the water, and I easily passed him. He emerged, sputtering, with pondweed hanging from one of his ears. And the archery contest? Well, let us say that my father needed a few more men to look after his growing herd of horses.

12   There were more suitors, and each challenged me to a different contest, but I beat them all. It seemed I could swim, run, ride, hunt, and fight better than any man. My parents were beginning to despair. My mother came to talk to me one evening as I was making new arrowheads.

13   "I cannot understand you," she began. "You are upsetting your father—he needs you to marry and forge an alliance with another tribe. Your sisters, too, are worried. They will soon come of a marriageable age, and they do want to marry. Men will not be interested in them if you do not stop your antics and find a husband."

14   At this I rolled my eyes. My mother was exaggerating, playing on my guilt to get her way. She continued, "Stop thinking about yourself, and think about your family. I realize you may be nervous about marriage, but you cannot put it off forever."

15   I turned away, and continued sharpening my arrowheads. My mother waited for a response, but I pretended to be too deeply absorbed in my task. I did not want her to see how deeply her words had cut me.

16   Three days later, a new man rode into our camp. He was immensely tall, and even I had to admit, very handsome. He

NOTICE: Photocopying any part of this book is forbidden by law.

215

walked with a swagger, and when he introduced himself as Batugu, I realized I had heard his name before. He was a Mongol from Iran, and he had proven his worth in battle with high distinction. But just the way he walked told me that his conceit had grown with his fame.

17   "Ah, Princess Aigiarn," he said heartily, "I have heard much of your little contests. But today you have met your future husband, and you can put an end to your games."

18   By now, a large crowd had gathered, and there were snickers and catcalls.

19   He now addressed my father. "Kaidu," he said, "I am so sure of victory that I will offer you, not 100 horses as a wager, but 1,000." A gasp went up from the crowd. "I choose, as my test of strength, wrestling." I began to feel nervous. The man was really big.

20   Preparations for the match began immediately. But before we wrestled, there was a feast. Batugu ate heartily, boasting to my father and the other men of his many glorious victories in battle. While Batugu filled himself with smoked venison and airag, the fermented mare's milk that is a favorite drink among soldiers, I sat and thought. I watched the way he dismissed my mother and ignored my sisters, the way he called all the attention in the room to himself.

21   I was still thinking when it was time for the match to begin. As we began to circle each other in the ring, my mother's words came back to me. "Stop thinking of yourself," she had said. I was trying, but it was difficult. True, it would make my father happy to finally have his eldest daughter married. I thought of the calm and wise Shining Moon woman he had pronounced me on the day of my birth. Could I be her? My mother would be delighted as well, though I don't think she had ever imagined me living as far away as Iran. But I could never be happy with this man. He was boastful and arrogant, and he would see me as a trophy rather than a living, breathing human being. I did not want to go off and live in the deserts of Iran, to sit in this man's ger and cook his meals. I thought of what my father had said to me, "I would not have you marry a man who was not at least your equal." I did not think this man was my equal, and I decided there and then that if I had any chance of beating Batugu, I would do it. Anyway, I thought wryly, any anger my parents might feel at my getting rid of this suitor would probably be offset by my winning them 1,000 horses.

22   Batugu made the first lunge, but I dived to the left and he stumbled past me. I saw at once that, although he would beat me if this were merely a test of strength, I was quicker and more flexible than he was. A stomach full of venison and airag wouldn't help him either. Still, if I let him get hold of me, I wouldn't have a chance. If I was to win this match, it must end quickly.

23   The next time Batugu lunged, I was ready for him. He tried for my legs, but his great height forced him to bend uncomfortably low, leaving his footing unstable. I took advantage of his weakness by tripping up his left foot as I dodged his attack. He fell to the ground, surprised and furious, and quickly pushed himself up with his hands. I doubled back, and as he was nearly up, I kicked his bloated stomach. He fell back down to one knee, gripping his stomach with one hand and balancing himself shakily with the other. I quickly struck his elbow, causing him to lose his balance and fall on his face. I wrenched his arm behind him, twisting his wrist inwards and violently jabbing my knuckles into the flesh below his armpit. He groaned and collapsed. I spun into the traditional Eagle Dance of victory, and the humiliated Batugu, as tradition also requires, had to get up and pass submissively under my outstretched, flapping arms. The crowd went wild with cheering and shouting, and I was gathered by burly warriors and held over their heads. Even my father could not contain his pride at my besting Iran's greatest hero. Only my mother and Batugu stayed away from the festive march, she retiring sadly into her ger, and he sulkily nursing his scratched face and wounded wrist.

24   Tomorrow will mark my twenty-fifth birthday, and I am still not married. Perhaps I never will take a husband. Then again, perhaps I will fall in love with a soldier, or the man who rides beside me in the next great hunt. Either way, I will follow my own heart in the matter.

©*Copyright 2002 by Jessica Wade.*
Reprinted by permission

Title IX

1   Open up the sports pages of the San Antonio Express-News or the Houston Chronicle. Depending on the time of year, you're likely to see a big article about Venus or Serena Williams winning yet another Grand Slam tennis championship. Or maybe you want to check on how the Houston Comets are doing. Are they still the best team in women's pro basketball?

2   Although you may not realize it today, it wasn't always so easy to find out about your favorite female professional athletes. Before Title IX became the law in 1972—and for a long time afterwards—you wouldn't have been able to follow your favorite women's basketball team. There weren't any. Until April 1996, there was no Women's National Basketball Association (WNBA), and the league's first games were not played until June 1997.

3   It took a federal law to pave the way for the WNBA and for other professional women's sports teams. That law was Title IX of the Education Amendments of 1972, which states:

4   *No person in the United States shall, on the basis of sex, be excluded from participation in, be denied the benefits of, or be subjected to discrimination under any program or activity receiving federal financial assistance.*

5   What exactly does this mean? Title IX makes it illegal to discriminate against anyone, students or employees, involved in education programs and activities that receive federal funds merely because of his or her gender. Why is Title IX so important? It is important because it is a very far-reaching law. Most schools receive some sort of federal funds (think of school lunch programs), so Title IX applies to almost every student in the country. That means that Title IX protects approximately 51.7 million elementary and secondary school students and approximately 14.4 million college and university students. It also protects the teachers and other people who work at those educational institutions.

6   Before Title IX, women did not have the same athletic or educational opportunities as men. Women were not eligible to receive athletic scholarships, not even women like Donna de Varona, a swimmer who won two gold medals for the United States in the 1964 Olympics. This put women at a real disadvantage, academically as well as athletically.

7   This disadvantage began to turn around after the passage of Title IX, as more and more girls began to participate in sports. As talented young girls started playing soccer, basketball, hockey, and other team sports, they learned new skills and gained confidence in their abilities. They showed that, with equal opportunities, girls do just as well as boys on the field, on the court, and on the rink. As softball pitcher and coach Lisa Fernandez, the pitcher for the gold-medal winning first United States Olympic softball team, explained: "I feel I have been a part of a general awakening that has occurred for women in sports since 1972. I had already competed at the high school, college, and International level for many years and was ready for the challenge of the [Olympics] tryouts and competitions." When asked about the impact of Title IX on her life, Sheryl Swoopes, WNBA All-Star member of the Houston Comets and another Olympic gold medal winner, replied: "Having the funds available for a basketball scholarship was a great blessing for me, or else I wouldn't have been able to go to college."

8   Over the past 30 years, girls and women have made significant strides toward equality in athletics. As more opportunities have opened up to them at all age levels, they have taken full advantage of all their new options. Today, more than 100,000 women participate in intercollegiate sports, four times more than participated in 1971. The numbers are even more striking at the high school level. In 1971, 300,000 girls took part in high school sports. By 1996, that number had grown to 2.4 million. According to John Romano, a writer for the St. Petersburg (FL) Times, "Because of Title IX, women's athletics enjoy a higher profile. Because of Title IX, girls can understand the joys of the playing field like never before."

9   Many people know that Title IX deals with equal opportunities in sports. But they often do not realize that Title IX applies to all aspects of education, from access to courses to school-sponsored extracurricular activities, from college recruitment and admissions to financial aid and scholarships.

10   Educational opportunities in this country were very different before Title IX became the law. High school girls could not sign up for courses like auto mechanics or wood shop—and boys could not take classes in home economics. Many educational

institutions had quotas that limited the number of women they would accept. To be admitted under this quota system, women usually had to have higher test scores and better grades than the men who were admitted to the same schools. When they were able to enroll in college, women who lived on campus were subjected to rules that the men did not have to follow, such as having to be in their dorm rooms by midnight. Many school and university buildings even had separate entrances for male and female students.

11   Look around you today, and you can see how different your life is from what it would have been before Title IX. Title IX eliminated many of the obstacles that used to keep girls and women from pursuing their chosen educational and career paths. In a speech marking the 25th anniversary of Title IX in 1997, Richard W. Riley, a former U.S. Secretary of Education, noted that "it seems fitting to suggest that America is a more equal, more educated and more prosperous nation because of the far-reaching effects of this legislation."

12   But these changes did not happen overnight, and they did not come easily. Many people, men and women, struggled to achieve the goal of equality. That struggle continues today. And all of us—girls and boys, women and men—reap the benefits.

Changes in Sex Ratios in Higher Education, 1972–1994

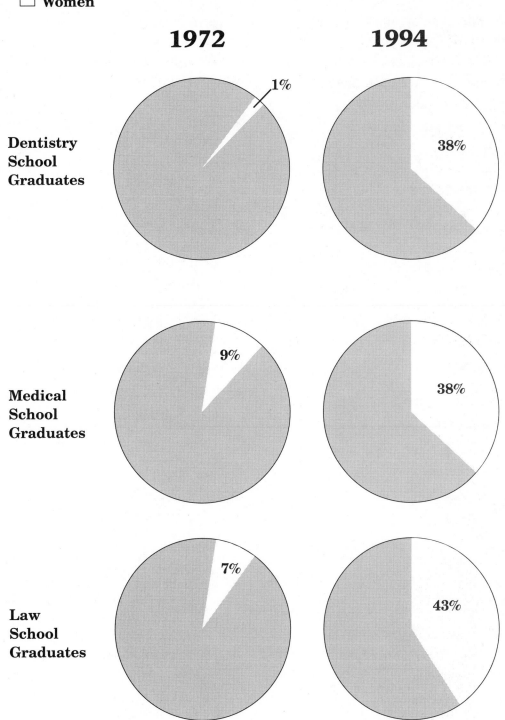

□ Men

□ Women

1972   **1994**

Dentistry
School
Graduates

1%

38%

Medical
School
Graduates

9%

38%

Law
School
Graduates

7%

43%

USE THE SELECTION "SHINING MOON"
(pp. 221-225) to answer questions 1–14.

1   This selection mostly deals with —

A   a family conflict between two ideas about the proper role of women

B   how a Persian warrior tried to win the hand of a Mongol princess

C   how Aigiarn led the Mongol soldiers in battle

D   the difficulty of preserving the traditional Mongol way of life

2   The name her father gave to Princess Aigiarn her shows that he expected her to be —

A   intelligent and inventive

B   lovely and gentle

C   strong and skillful

D   witty and amusing

3   What especially inspired Aigiarn when she was a young girl?

A   The achievements of her great-great grandfather

B   The advice of her mother

C   The friendship of the men

D   The reputation of her father

4   What does the reader learn about Kaidu in this selection?

A   He is a rash and reckless leader.

B   He is determined to choose his daughter's husband.

C   He is old and getting weak.

D   He is proud of his daughter's unconventional accomplishments.

5   How do the soldiers of Aigiarn's people react to her hunting and fighting skills?

A   They shun her because she does not represent the traditional female role.

B   They want her to marry Batugu to forge a trade alliance with his powerful tribe.

C   They respect her abilities and treat her as one of their own.

D   They ask her to lead them into battle against the Mongols of Iran.

6   What techniques does Aigiarn's mother use to try to persuade her to marry?

A   anger and disgust

B   guilt and exaggeration.

C   logic and reasoning

D   ordering and threatening punishment

7   Which of the following is the best summary of the selection? ?

A   As a child, the Mongol Princess Aigiarn accompanied the men of her tribe on hunts, and when she grew up she also rode into battle with her father. She was the equal of any man in feats of strength and skill. Both her father and the men of her tribe admired her, but they also felt that she should get married and assume the traditional role of a woman.

B Princess Shining Moon refused to marry anyone unless they could beat her in a wrestling match. She wrestled many suitors and beat them all. One that he defeated was a huge, arrogant suitor from Iran named Batugu, and she beat him by using her quickness rather than her strength.

C Shining Moon, a Mongol Princess, grew up to be the equal of any man in her tribe in hunting, fighting, and other activities that were ordinarily the province of the men. When her parents insisted that she marry, she agreed on the condition that her husband must be able to beat her in some feat of strength or skill. Many tried, including a huge warrior named Batugu, but none succeeded, and she reached her twenty-fifth birthday still unmarried.

D The Mongol people originally lived in dry and treeless lands. They became a conquering people when led by a leader named Chinggis Khan. Eventually they conquered from China to Europe. But many of them still kept to the old ways, living on horseback and in felt tents.

8 In paragraph 9, *My father was silent for a moment, but then a small smile spread across his face* indicates that —

A Kaidu has thought of a way to trick Aigiarn into getting married

B Kaidu hopes that Aigiarn will defeat most of her competitors and prove that women are superior to men

C Kaidu is pleased that Aigiarn will marry according to Mongol custom

D Kaidu is amused by Aigiarn's solution; it respects both her parents' wishes and her own, and if she does not marry, it will increase his herd of horses

9 In paragraph 16, which word helps you understand what kind of walk a *swagger* is?

A *conceit*

B *distinction*

C *handsome*

D *worth*

10 Why does Batugu wager 1,000 horses instead of 100?

A He has to, because he comes from a different tribe

B He wants Aigiarn and her father to like and admire him.

C He wants to show how confident he is.

D He wants to show how very rich he is.

11 What is paragraph 21 mainly about?

A Aigiarn's desire to win Batugu's horses for her parents.

B Aigiarn's dislike of the boastful Batugu.

C Aigiarn's plans on how to win the wrestling match

D the conflict between Aigiarn's desire to please her parents and her need to be true to herself

223

12 In paragraph 21, "he would see me as a trophy rather than a living, breathing human being" indicates that—

A Aigiarn wins every contest she enters.

B Batugu wants to marry Aigiarn because he loves her.

C Aigiarn is very beautiful, and he will put her on a throne.

D Batugu wants to marry Aigiarn to show everyone that he is stronger and more powerful than she is.

13 What common saying best summarizes the point the author makes when she describes Batugu's preparations for the wrestling match?

A "Pride goeth before a fall."

B "Haste makes waste."

C "Don't judge a book by its cover."

D "Every cloud has a silver lining."

14 Suppose Aigiarn wanted to add one more sentence to the end of her story. Which one would she most probably add?

A *How I live will be my own choice.*

B *I suppose I'll have to give in to my mother's wishes some day.*

C *I will probably marry a soldier from Iran to ensure the wealth and security of my tribe.*

D *I'll never marry, because men are weak.*

USE THE SELECTION "TITLE IX" (pp. 226-228) to answer questions 15-28.

15 Title IX of the Education Amendments of 1972 is a federal law that prohibits discrimination based on —

A age

B gender

C race

D national origin

16 If discrimination is made illegal, the result is—

A equality of opportunity

B favoritism

C friendship

D toleration

17 Which of the following statements is most accurate?

A Title IX applies principally to girls and women who play sports.

B Title IX applies to education programs that receive federal funding.

C Title IX applies to male and female high school students only.

D Title IX requires colleges to provide scholarships for all women.

18 In paragraph 6, what does *"Because of Title IX, girls can understand the joys of the playing field like never before"* mean?

   A More girls play baseball and soccer than all other sports combined.

   B Opportunities for girls to participate in sports have increased during the past 30 years.

   C Title IX has created complete equality for girls and boys who participate in sports.

   D Newspapers devote more space to reporting on women's sports.

19 Under an educational *quota system* —

   A all admission applications are reviewed without regard to the applicant's religion, gender, or race

   B colleges and universities admit a specified, limited number of people from a particular religious, gender, or racial group

   C equal numbers of men and women are admitted to colleges and universities

   D only the people with the highest grade point averages are eligible to receive college degrees

20 What does it mean in paragraph 11 when former Secretary of Education Riley suggests that *"America is a more equal, more educated and more prosperous nation because of the far-reaching effects"* of Title IX?

   A All American children now participate in organized after-school sports programs.

   B American colleges and universities accept every high school graduate who applies for admission.

   C More educational and well-paying career opportunities are available to women and men than were available before Title IX became law.

   D Teachers have received major pay raises under Title IX, so they can afford to buy more cars and bigger houses.

21 Read the following dictionary entry:

subject 1: to be obedient to **2**: to cause to undergo or experience **3**: to be bound by loyalty or allegiance to **4**: the doer of the action of a sentence

Which definition best matches the meaning of the word *subjected* as it is used in paragraph 4 of the selection?

   A Definition 1

   B Definition 2

   C Definition 3

   D Definition 4

22 Which event or events of the 1960's foreshadowed the passage of Title IX?

   A The assassination of President Kennedy

   B The Civil Rights movement for racial equality

   C The rise of rock groups

   D The Vietnam War

23 What is paragraph 5 mainly about?

   A how Title IX protects teachers

   B school lunch programs

   C the kinds of discrimination in education that women used to face

   D the scope of Title IX

24 Read the following dictionary entry:

profile 1: a side view   **2**: to a concise description   **3**: a graph of a person's abilities, as determined by tests   **4**: a degree or level of exposure to the public

Which definition best matches the meaning of the word *profile* as it is used in the next-to last sentence of paragraph 8 of the selection?

A   Definition 1

B   Definition 2

C   Definition 3

D   Definition 4

25 How does the author support her contention that Title IX has been influential in women's sports?

A   by comparing women's participation in sports before and after the passage of the act

B   by giving reasons why increased women's participation in sports is a good thing

C   by showing how much money female sports figures have made through product endorsements

D   by showing how women have become much better than men at sports

26 What is one way in which Title IX improved educational opportunities for women?

A   It compelled women's colleges to improve their standards.

B   It ended the quota system, which imposed higher standards for college admissions on women than on men.

C   It forced colleges to accept any woman who applied.

D   It channeled federal money into women's studies.

27 What is another way in which Title IX improved educational opportunities for women?

A   It changed the rules for dormitory living.

B   It instituted special courses for women in high schools

C   It made women eligible for athletic scholarships to college.

D   It set up a system of preparing women for higher education

28 Which of the following people is most likely to be protected by Title IX?

A   a young man who has problems on in college buildings because he is in a wheelchair

B   a young man who wants to become a chef and applies for cooking classes.

C   an African American computer technician applying for promotion

D   an elderly man of 70 who wants to go to law school

USE "SHINING MOON: A RETELLING" AND "TITLE IX"
to answer questions 29 and 30.

---

29 The most important difference between opportunities for Aigiarn and for American girls growing up in the past 30 years is that —

A Aigiarn lived in ancient Mongolia; Title IX applies only in the United States.

B Aigiarn challenged men to contests of physical power; girls today play on the same sports teams as boys.

C Aigiarn was a princess who could do whatever she wanted to do; there is no royal family in the United States.

D Aigiarn had to create her own opportunities to lead a nontraditional life; Title IX helps to create those kinds of opportunities.

30 An important difference between Aigiarn and women athletes of today is that —

A Agiarn was not admired, whereas women athletes today are.

B Aigiarn competed against men; women athletes of today customarily compete against other women.

C Aigiarn started her athletic career when young, whereas modern women athletes do not.

D Aigiarn was a soldier, whereas modern women athletes never are.

USE THE VISUAL REPRESENTATION ON PAGE 221
to answer questions 31 and 32.

---

31 What is the primary purpose of these circle graphs?

A They show the relative increase in female dental, medical, and law school graduates since Title IX became law.

B They show the increased enrollment in dental, medical, and law school since Title IX became law.

C They compare the absolute numbers of male and female dental, medical, and law school graduates since Title IX became law.

D They show the increase in female dental, medical, and law school applicants since Title IX became law.

32 In which profession did the percentage of female graduates increase the *least* between 1972 and 1994?

A dentistry

B medicine

C law

D need more information

OPEN-ENDED ITEMS

33   In "Shining Moon," what is Batugu's opinion of Aigiarn's achievements? Support your answer with evidence from the selection.

_____

_____

_____

_____

34   What do you think is the most important effect that Title IX has had on women in addition to encouraging women's athletics? Support your answer with evidence from the selection.

_____

_____

_____

_____

35   Both Aigiarn and the women athletes of today received some encouragement and support. In each case, where did it come from? Support your answer with evidence from the selection.

_____

_____

_____

_____

WRITTEN COMPOSITION

> **Write a composition explaining why creating or taking advantage of opportunities is an important part of life.**

The information in the box below will help you remember what you should think about when you write your composition.

REMEMBER—YOU SHOULD

- **write about the assigned topic**

- **make your writing thoughtful and interesting**

- **make sure that each sentence you write contributes to the composition as a whole**

- **make sure that your ideas are clear and easy for the reader to follow**

- **write about your ideas in depth so that the reader is able to develop a good understanding of what you are**

- **proofread your writing to correct errors in spelling, capitalization, punctuation, grammar, and sentence structure**

Revising and Editing—Selection 1

Below is an article written for the back-to-school edition of the Rayburn Remarker, Sam Rayburn High School's school newspaper. Help prepare it for publication by reading it carefully and answering the questions that follow.

Get Ready for This Year's Rayburn Raiders!

[1] This fall at Sam Rayburn High School, everyone is excited. [2] Football season is around the corner, and we have a great team this year. [3] "This just might be our best year ever," Millard Fullbright, the coach, told the Rayburn Remarker. [4] There have been many great Rayburn Raiders in the past, this year Coach Fullbright may be right.

[5] Our quarterback this year will be senior Brian Singleton. [6] Singleton is a powerful athlete at the top of his game he has wanted to be quarterback since he started playing for Rayburn High. [7] He is getting his chance to be the team's leader. [8] And how does he feel about the big responsibility on his shoulders. [9] "I feel good," says Singleton. [10] "I've practiced very hard, and I'm confident I can lead our team to victory."

[11] The rest of the offensive players are just as confident. [12] Lineman Ricky Guiterez took time out from his wait training to speak with the Remarker. [13] "The linemen have been training all summer," Guiterez says. [14] "We can't wait to use what we've been practicing!" [15] They had better watch out!

[16] The Raider's defense is very promising this year as well. [17] We watched defensive backs during a recent practice Lonnie Thomas and Ralph Smathers. [18] Practice is held every day from 3:30 to 6 P.M. [19] Both of these juniors run so fast it's impossible to keep up with them. [20] "Nobody will get past our defensive line," says Coach Fullbright, with a smile.

[21] Football season is indeed just around the corner, and our Rayburn Raiders are ready. [22] Here at the Remarker, all we can say is: Are you ready? [23] If you're not ready yet. [24] You'd better get ready fast. [25] Its going to be one exciting fall.

1   What change, if any, should be made in sentence 4?

   A   Change *There* to **There**

   B   Insert the word **but** after the comma

   C   Change *Coach Fullbright* to **coach Fullbright**

   D   Make no change

2 What change should be made in sentence 6?

  A Change *athlete* to **athelete**

  B Insert a semicolon after *game*

  C Change *has* to **had**

  D Change *Rayburn High* to **Rayburn high**

3 What transition should be added to the beginning of sentence 7?

  A However,

  B Therefore,

  C Finally,

  D Even so,

4 What change needs to be made in sentence 8?

  A Change *does* to **do**

  B Insert a comma after **feel**

  C Change *his* to **their**

  D Change the period to a question mark

5 What change should be made in sentence 12?

  A Change *Lineman* to **Line man**

  B Insert commas after *Guiterez* and *training*

  C Change *wait* to **weight**

  D Change *training* to **trains**

6 The meaning of sentence 15 can be clarified by changing *They* to —

  A The other teams

  B The offensive players

  C Them

  D Singleton and Guiterez

7 What is the most effective way to improve the organization of the fourth paragraph (sentences 16–20)?

  A Move sentence 16 to the end of the paragraph

  B Move sentence 18 to the end of the paragraph

  C Delete sentence 18

  D Delete sentence 20

8 What is the most effective way to rewrite sentence 17?

  A During a recent practice, Lonnie Thomas watched defensive back Ralph Smathers.

  B We watched, defensive backs Lonnie Thomas and Ralph Smathers, during a recent practice.

  C Lonnie Thomas and Ralph Smathers, defensive backs, we watched during a recent practice.

  D During a recent practice, we watched defensive backs Lonnie Thomas and Ralph Smathers.

9 What is the most effective way to rewrite the ideas in sentences 23 and 24?

  A If you're not ready yet; you'd better get ready fast.

  B If you're not ready yet, you'd better get ready fast.

  C You're not ready yet. You'd better get ready fast.

  D Yet you're better, not ready, if you get ready fast.

10 What change, if any, should be made in sentence 25?

  A Change *Its* to **It's**

  B Change *going* to **gone**

  C Change *one* to **an**

  D Make no change

Revising and Editing—Selection 2

Robert Nuncies wrote the essay below for a class on the history of mathematics. Help him make the essay stronger by reading it carefully and answering the questions that follow.

Sophie Germain

[1] In 1789, when the French Revolution was beginning, a young woman was also getting ready to create a revolution, who was named Sophie Germain. [2] Sophie Germain was 13 years old, and she had just discovered mathematics. [3] People were fighting in the streets of Paris, but she sat in her fathers library and read every book about mathematics that she could find. [4] No one knew then how far she would go in the world.

[5] In those days, people believed that it was dangerous for a girl's health if she studies too much. [6] Sophie Germain's parents tried to keep her from studying by doing things like not giving her any candles to keep her from reading at night. [7] But Sophie always found a way to study anyway, she kept candles hidden in her room and took them out after her parents had gone to bed. [8] Finally, her parents gave up and let Sophie study as much as she wanted.

[9] Women couldn't be students at the Ecole Polytechnique. [10] The Ecole Polytechnique was a university where many great mathematicians taught. [11] Sophie had to borrow notes from the male students. [12] She also had to turn in papers under someone else's name. [13] The work she did got the attention of the university's top professor, who found out that she was actually a woman. [14] Instead of getting upset, he came to see her and encouraged her to keep studying. [15] The French Revolution had ended by then.

[16] Sophie also pretended to be a man when she wrote to the well-known German mathematician Karl Friedrich Gauss. [17] They wrote to each other for several years. [18] Before Gauss found out that Sophie was a woman.

[19] Sophie Germain spent her whole life studying mathematics. [20] She did important research in number theory. [21] The work she did in physics on the theory of elasticity helped make possible the construction of the Eiffel Tower. [22] When the

Eiffel Tower was built, the names of 72 men whose knowledge and research contributed to this engineering feat were engraved on the structure.

[23] Sophie Germain's name was not mentioned. [24] She was still invisible in the world of mathematics then. [25] She is now considered one of the founders of mathematical physics.

---

1 What is the most effective way to rewrite sentence 1?

A When a young woman who was named Sophie Germain in 1789, was getting ready to create a revolution, the French Revolution was also beginning.

B When the French Revolution was beginning in 1789, a young woman was also getting ready to create a revolution, who was named Sophie Germain.

C In 1789, a young woman was also getting ready to create a revolution when the French Revolution was beginning, who was named Sophie Germain.

D In 1789, when the French Revolution was beginning, a young woman named Sophie Germain was also getting ready to create a revolution.

2 What change should be made in sentence 3?

A Change *were fighting* to **are fought**

B Change *fathers* to **father's**

C Insert a comma after *library*

D Change *could find* to **found**

3 What change, if any, should be made in sentence 5?

A Change *believed* to **believe**

B Change *was* to **is**

C Change *studies* to **studied**

D Make no change

4 What change should be made in sentence 7?

A Insert commas after *but* and **study**

B Change the comma after *anyway* to a semicolon

C Insert a comma after *room*

D Change *took* to **would take**

5 What is the most effective way to combine sentences 9 and 10?

A Students at the Ecole Polytechnique, a university, couldn't be women where many great mathematicians taught.

B A university where many great mathematicians taught, the Ecole Polytechnique, women couldn't be students.

C Women couldn't be students at the Ecole Polytechnique, a university where many great mathematicians taught.

D A university where many great mathematicians taught, women couldn't be students at the Ecole Polytechnique.

6 What is the most effective way to improve the organization of the third paragraph (sentences 9–15)?

    A Move sentence 11 between sentences 12 and 13   .

    B Delete sentence 12

    C Move sentence 14 to the end of the paragraph

    D Delete sentence 15

7 What is the most effective way to rewrite the ideas in sentences 17 and 18?

    A They wrote to each other for several years before Gauss found out that Sophie was a woman.

    B They wrote to each other for several years, before Gauss found out that Sophie was a woman.

    C Before Gauss found out that Sophie was a woman; they wrote to each other for several years.

    D Before Gauss found out that Sophie was a woman for several years, they wrote to each other.

8 Which of these sentences could be added to the end of the fourth paragraph (sentences 16–18) to support the ideas in that paragraph?

    A Later, Sophie would do important work on the Eiffel Tower.

    B The deception was necessary because people back then simply would not take a female mathematician seriously.

    C Gauss knew the reputation of the Ecole Polytechnique, of course.

    D Several of their letters are very interesting to read.

9 What transition should be added to the beginning of sentence 23?

    A Therefore,

    B Before,

    C Even then,

    D Finally,

10 What change, if any, should be made in sentence 25?

    A Change *is* to **was**

    B Change *founders* to **funders**

    C Change *mathematical physics* to **Mathematical Physics**

    D Make no change

Practice Test 2

Read the two selections and the viewing and representing piece. Then answer the questions that follow.

The Race

By David Fernandez

1   *Let's go, let's go, no way is he going to beat me this time, I have to hold on.* We shot around the turn and I opened up my stride, but I could still feel Danny coming behind me. Danny pulled away effortlessly and was already out of reach. He crossed the line a full three seconds before me, all of which he had gained on the last lap. The rest of the squad came in after us and collapsed where they finished, heaving as they caught their breath. Danny was breathing a little heavily, but he seemed unfazed. He held out a hand for me. "Good run, man. I swear, I'm going to be so glad in two weeks, when I'll be done with cross-country forever. I'll see you later." I nodded, breathing too heavily to speak, and he turned, walking towards the locker room.

2   Two weeks—the season was nearly over, and we had just two weeks before the State Championships in Madison. It would be my last cross-country meet in high school, and possibly my last ever. This was supposed to be the big year when I could define myself as a runner, when I could show colleges that I had a future, when I could break out from being a decent leg on a relay with Danny to being a runner worth having for myself. It seemed like I had just kept putting it off—there had been so many other problems this year, college applications, my community service requirement, and worst of all, physics. They all took a toll on running, my season just slipping away from me day by day.

3   I wished so much that I could have legs like Danny's, legs that made every race seem effortless. He hated cross-country, preferring the easier time he had with competition in short sprints, where his natural ability could carry him. Cross-country was my favorite for that same reason—I could stay with most runners, even with my modest talent, because the difficulty of the course and the length of the race served as an equalizer. I suppose cross-country appeals to a side of me that loves to have everything well planned out. It is very easy to lose track of the race and get winded early on, and a lot of people do that when the course is a difficult one. For some people it does not matter one way or the other, but it could still make all the difference for me.

Danny would definitely have a scholarship, wherever he went, but if I could beat him in just one race, I might be able to get one, too.

4   I looked over at his locker, which he had plastered with all his offers and pleas from colleges all around the country. Georgetown, Arkansas, Stanford—my pile at home was far less impressive, and almost none of the brochures I had received contained information about running.

5   "It's really hard to pick, you know, José? They all seem so awesome."

6   "Yeah, I guess."

7   "This one guy," pointing at a letter closer to the bottom of the locker, "has called me about a million times. He's totally annoying."

8   I bobbed my head in agreement, and threw my clothes in a bag. "Listen, I'll see you tomorrow, Danny. I had better get going."

9   "Sure, see you later, José."

10   It was already completely dark when I left the locker room, and the ice from last week's snowstorm was dirty and hard on the sidewalk. As usual, physics was hard and took me forever. I went to bed tired, knowing I was going to wake up tired the following day.

11   The two weeks flew by, and when we finally warmed up in Madison I felt better than I had expected to—maybe it was because Danny hadn't said anything on the way upstate. As we stretched to stay warm in the twenty-degree cold, I felt calm, knowing that all the preparations were out of my hands. There was just the race left.

12   I had borrowed my brother's car for a day to go to the course so I could plan out my race, visualizing it the whole way. Madison was nothing like the gentle hills of the Lake Park golf course we ran on most weekends. It began with a mile in the open on flat ground, then some rolling hills with a huge hill right in the middle. It was a fearsome dark mass, and the path of the course was black and muddy where it had been churned up by runners in previous races. Once past

that, though, it was a flat half-mile leading up to the finish line, so once I cleared that my plan would have to be give it everything, holding nothing back.

13   "The race will start in five minutes."

14   Danny and I began to take off our warm-up clothes, and jog a little bit more. We took our places on the line, approximately dead in the middle of about three hundred and fifty runners. Danny slapped me on the back, and said, "All right, let's do this."

15   "Yeah, man, it's the last one, you and me," I said.

16   "On your marks—set—" The gun went off and the line exploded forward.

17   The mile of open space made many people feel that they needed to really push it at the start, especially since this was the State Championships. Danny settled in with the front pack, and I hung in the middle, trying not to fall too far behind, and trying not to become too tired. Sure enough, several of the runners who were fastest off the line were definitely slowing down, and I was gaining ground. I was set, so far.

18   The rolling hills created a bottleneck, and it started to get ugly, as runners threw elbows and punches to get a better position in the crowd. I was able to find a small bit of trail to the side that seemed miraculously wide open, and cut in front. I could see the front pack, with Danny in the middle. It looked like even he was having a hard time, and it seemed as though he was slipping back, not used to the rough and tumble, or to having other people that good to run with. I couldn't believe it—my plan was working, and I had a shot to move up on Danny and the front pack, if I could just keep them close enough by the time I made it to that hill.

19   We made two sharp right turns, and as the path curved back to the left I could see the hill in the corner of my eye. I had to make up some ground now, and then surge just as I was approaching the top, when most people slow down. The hill became very steep very quickly, and had several areas where the path could hold two runners, side by side, at most. I saw Danny not too far in front of me at one of these tiny bottlenecks, and two runners cut him off, the second giving him a fairly brutal shove into the tree. I heard an unnatural crack, and saw Danny hunched over.

NOTICE: Photocopying any part of this book is forbidden by law.

237

20   "Danny, are you all right?" He didn't respond, just seemed to be groaning there. I was yelling while running, so he might not have heard me. I wanted to go to him, but I knew my plan would come apart if I did that, and probably ruin the best race of my life. But maybe Danny was just shaken, and needed a hand, and besides, he needed this much more than I did—I might be fine getting into college with my grades, but he would not. Then again, he might be more hurt than I could help, and by going to get help as fast as I could I'd be helping him more. It seemed like there were a thousand possibilities, and he came closer with each step I took.

21   As I came nearer, I got a better look at him. He had stopped moving entirely, just totally still. There was no way he would get up, even if he were not hurt badly—he was falling off his pace, near my pack and was probably going to give up anyway. He never had any will power when his ability could not carry him, and I would just be wasting time with him. He would not have stopped if I was on the ground instead. I kept going, and surged over the hill, watching the front pack still close ahead of me.

22   I dashed down the slope, just letting my legs go as fast as they could. It seemed like I never got any closer to the front pack, which I could have expected. I made it to the last half mile and started to open up, but without strategy it was not long until I was passed by a couple of people. I suppose I finished well enough. As I passed the finish line, the realization that my season was over hit me. My time, while better, was still close to where I had been, and my unlikely hope for a scholarship faded. My coach ran over and asked about Danny, and I told him what happened. He ran off, and soon an ambulance was flying across the field. Danny met it at the base of the hill, having gotten up and walked the rest of the way. We did not say a single thing to each other the whole way home.

© 2002 David Fernandez Reprinted by permission

A Fire Captain's Eulogy

by Captain James Gormley

The building housing Engine Company 40 and Ladder Company 35 is on the corner of Amsterdam Avenue and 66th Street, and because it is on the West Side, its men managed to get to the World Trade Center disaster sooner than many other units. Of the 13 firefighters who jumped aboard the two rigs that morning, only one survived, Kevin Shea, who was apparently knocked unconscious during the collapse of one of the towers and literally blown out of the building.

In the weeks and months that followed, the men of the firehouse attended a series of services for their fallen comrades from this and other units. At the last of these services for the men of 40/35, on Dec. 10, Capt. James Gormley, the house commander, paid tribute to his colleague, Capt. Francis J. Callahan, a 30-year veteran of the department who was killed on Sept. 11. Captain Gormley eloquently described the complexity of command facing an officer in the New York Fire Department. His eulogy was delivered, fittingly, at Alice Tully Hall at Lincoln Center, for which the firefighters of 40/35 had been responsible.

1   Captains and lieutenants of the New York City Fire Department share a special relationship with other officers of similar rank. When we meet for the first time we introduce ourselves to each other, we shake hands, we measure each other's resolve and fortitude. At Operations our aggressiveness is based on the trust we share in each other.

2   Firefighters and their officers share a different, but also special relationship. Officers very literally lead firefighters into harm's way. We go first. If things go badly we are required by our oath and tradition to be the last of our command to leave. Accountability for our men is carved into our heart. Responsibility for our men, their wives and children are in the depth of our soul.

3   This is why we are here today. Capt. Frank Callahan is the ranking officer killed at the World Trade Center from our firehouse. He leaves last. I cannot say he will be the last to ever leave. We live in a dangerous world, and we put our boots and helmets on every day.

4   Captains, especially commanding officers of companies in the same quarters, have a unique relationship. We know each other as no one else ever will. We are commanding officers of complementary companies. We cannot work successfully without each other. There are not many of us, you could fit us in one fair-sized room. We are not always friends. There is too much at stake, but our respect, and trust in each other, is unquestioned.

5   Frank Callahan was more than my friend, To simply call him brother would not do our relationship justice. Frank was my

comrade. It's harder to be a comrade than a friend. It's different than being a brother.

6   Friends and brothers forgive your mistakes. They are happy to be with you. You can relax and joke with them. You can take your ease with them—tell them tall tales.

7   Comrades are different. Comrades forgive nothing. They can't. They need you to be better. They keep you sharp. They take your words literally.

8   When a friend dies we miss them, we regret words unspoken, we remember the love. When a brother dies we grieve for the future without him. His endless possibilities. If your brother doesn't die of old age you might never accept the parting. When a comrade dies we miss them, we regret words unspoken, we remember the love, we grieve the future without them. We are also proud. Proud to have known a good man, a better man than ourselves. We respect the need for him to leave, to rest.

9   Some people equate camaraderie with being jovial. It is anything but. Camaraderie is sharing hardship. It is shouts and commands, bruises, and cuts. It's a sore back and lungs that burn from exertion. It's heat on your neck and a pit in your stomach. It's a grimy handshake and a hug on wet shoulders when we're safe. It's not being asleep when it's your turn on watch. It is trust, it is respect, it is acting honorably.

10   You hold your comrade up when he can't stand on his own. You breathe for him when his body's forgotten how. It's lifting a man up who loves his wife and children as much as you love your own. Looking them in the eye for the rest of your life and trying to explain, and not being able to. You kiss them for him. It's laying him down gently when his name appears on God's roll call. It's remembering his name. I'll never forget his name. He was just what he was called: Frank. You never had to chase your answer. He said it to your face.

11   It's at the same time being both amazed and proud that you've known men like him. Looking for your reflection in their image. Seeing it. Knowing you're one of them.

12   There's a song out of Ireland. A line of it says, "Comrade tread lightly, you're near to a hero's grave." If you ever said that to Frank he would have given you the "look" and pushed past you in the hallway.

13   Frank was light on his feet but he never tread anywhere lightly. When Frank did something it was like a sharp axe biting into soft fresh pine, with a strong sure stroke. It was done. It was right. It meant something. It was refreshing. It smelled good.

14   Quite often we discussed history. The successes and failures of political, military and social leadership. The depth and broadness of Frank's historical knowledge was astounding.

15   I've been told Frank enjoyed a practical joke. We never joked together. Rarely laughed. We never sought out each other's company on days off. We never went golfing or fishing. We never went for a hike in the Shawangunk Mountains together. We were often happier apart than we ever were together because we shared the nightmares of command.

16   We shared problems. We shared stress. We shared dark thoughts that are now front-page news. Incredulous at the failures of leadership that have borne fruit. We shared the proposition of a time and place where few would dare to go. He went there because it was his turn. He called his wife, Angie, before he received his orders to respond. He told her what was going on. He told her things didn't look good; he told her he loved her. Historically it is said, "they rode to the sound of the guns:"

Capt. Frank Callahan

Lt. John Ginley

Firefighter 1 Gr. Bruce Gary

Firefighter 1 Gr. James Giberson

Firefighter 1 Gr. Michael Otten

Firefighter 1 Gr. Kevin Bracken

Firefighter 1 Gr. Steve Mercado

Firefighter 1 Gr. Michael Roberts

Firefighter 1 Gr. John Marshall

Firefighter 3 Gr. Vincent Morello

Firefighter 3 Gr. Michael Lynch

Firefighter 6 Gr. Michael D'Auria

and Firefighter 2 Gr. Kevin Shea

17   Kevin, we are joyful that we got you back. Have no guilt. The same goes for the rest of us. I know what you all did, you got your gear on, found a tool, wrote your name or Social Security number in felt tip pen on your arm or a leg, a crisis tattoo in case you got found.

18   We went down there knowing things could go badly. We stayed until we were exhausted, got three hours sleep and went back again, and again. That's what comrades do. Only luck and circumstance separate us from them.

19   It is significant that we are in Lincoln Center for the Performing Arts. The first performance here was "West Side Story," the story of this neighborhood. This Act is part of that story. It is more than we can absorb in one lifetime, so the story must be told until it makes sense.

20   It is poignant because the arts have helped mankind deal with reality since stories were told round the fire and we drew on cave walls. The arts help us exercise our emotions. We are surrounded by art and overwhelmed by our emotions. From the pictures children have drawn for us, the poetry, songs, and banners, to the concerts, plays and operas that we have been invited to attend—use the arts to heal your heart. Exercise your emotions. Feel anger, feel hate, feel love and pride. Run the gamut of your emotions until you settle where you belong, as good honorable men, every inch the equal of our comrades, friends and brothers. That's what they want. That's what your families need. That's what you deserve.

21   Frank was a trusted leader, a captain. The best commander I've encountered here, or in the military. It was important to him. We both believed captain to be the most important rank in the department. He was forged by his family, his comrades, every officer and firefighter that he ever worked with. He was tempered by his experience.

22   History, the record of successes and failures of leadership, has caused us to be here. Capt. Frank Callahan did not fail in his leadership. He led his command where they were needed, and he's the last of them to leave. If more of the world's leaders were forged as he was, our world would not be in its current state.

23   Frank Callahan is a star, a reference point. A defined spot on the map of humanity. Guide on him to navigate the darkness. You will not wander, you will not become lost.

LA CUESTA HIGH SCHOOL
STUDENT COUNCIL
"Students helping students"

Scared you might
not graduate?

Classes not quite
this simple?

Need a better way
to get help?

YOUR STUDENT COUNCIL HAS A STUDY BUDDY FOR YOU! GET HELP FROM SENIORS WHO HAVE ALREADY PASSED YOUR COURSES!

Meet your Study Buddy on—
THURSDAY, January 27, and FRIDAY, January 18
THE SCHOOL LIBRARY
3 PM – 5 PM

USE "THE RACE"
(pp. 243-246) to answer questions 1–14.

1   Read the following dictionary entry:

surge (serj), **1**: to rise and fall like a wave **2**: to rise up suddenly to an abnormal height or value **3**: to sweep forward with increasing speed **4**: to let go a rope or slacken it gradually

Which definition best matches the meaning of the word *surge* as it is used in paragraph 19 of the story?

   A   Definition 1

   B   Definition 2

   C   Definition 3

   D   Definition 4

2   What is the most important conflict that José experiences in this story?

   A   his competing interests in his friendship with Danny and in his future

   B   his competing interests in running and schoolwork

   C   his competition against the other runners at the championship

   D   his conflict between staying with running or just quitting altogether

3   Why is José so eager to win the race?

   A   He wants people to see him as a champion.

   B   He wants to do his personal best.

   C   He wants to humble Danny.

   D   He wants to improve his chances of getting into college.

4   José's feeling for Danny can be best described as —

   A   a mixture of friendship and envy

   B   admiration and hero-worship

   C   deep affection alternating with anger and rage

   D   guarded dislike and contempt

5   In paragraph 12, the author includes information about José's surveying the course beforehand in order to —

   A   foreshadow the unfortunate events of the race

   B   show that José has lots of extra time on his hands

   C   show that José is afraid that he is not good enough to win the race

   D   show José's thoughtful approach to cross-country racing

6   Which paragraph shows a flashback?

   A   Paragraph 4

   B   Paragraph 10

   C   Paragraph 12

   D   Paragraph 15

7   In paragraph 21, José is shown to be thinking, "He never had any will power where his ability could not carry him, and I would just be wasting time with him." This can best be considered —

   A   a realistic and sensible assessment of Danny's character

   B   A rehearsal of what José has to say to the coach

   C   foreshadowing the loss of the race by both runners

   D   José's excuse to make himself feel better about his choice

8 How does Danny react to the letters he receives from different colleges?

   A He is annoyed and somewhat disgusted by all the attention.

   B He is excited and pleased by the letters.

   C He is hurt and disappointed by what the letters say.

   D He shows off the letters, but pretends to be unimpressed by them.

9 In which quotation from the selection does José show a glimpse of optimism?

   A *I went to bed tired, knowing I was going to wake up tired the following day"* (paragraph 10)

   B *It seemed like I never got closer to the front pack, which I could have expected.* (paragraph 22)

   C *Sure enough, several of the runners who were fastest off the line were definitely slowing down, and I was gaining ground.* (paragraph 17)

   D *They all took a toll on running, my season just slipping away from me day by day* (paragraph 2)

10 Which quotation from the selection does not show José's envy of Danny?

   A *Georgetown, Duke, Stanford—my pile at home was far less impressive, and almost none of the brochures I had received contained information about running.* (paragraph 4)

   B *I could show colleges that I had a future, when I could break out from being a decent leg on a relay with Danny to being a runner worth having for myself.* (paragraph 2)

   C *I might be fine getting into college with my grades, but he would not.* (paragraph 20)

   D *I wished so much that I could have legs like Danny's, legs that made every race seem effortless.* (paragraph 3)

11 What is the main idea of paragraph 1?

   A Danny and the narrator are best friends.

   B Danny enjoys cross-country racing.

   C Danny is a better runner than the narrator.

   D Danny is a poor sport.

12 What is the main theme of the selection?

   A how a competitive friendship can be tested

   B how an athletic scholarship can get you into a good college

   C how important it is to get a good education

   D how planning a cross-country race is important

13 What is the principal means that the narrator uses to do well in his races?

   A doing intensive workouts

   B following the advice of his coach

   C relying on natural ability

   D strategizing and planning ahead of time

14 Read the following dictionary entry:

leg, **1**: the limb of a human or an animal, used for support **2**: a pole or a bar used for support, especially on furniture **3**: the side of a right triangle that is not the hypotenuse **4**: a section of a race involving teams of runners running serially

Which definition best matches the meaning of the word *leg* as it is used in paragraph 2 of the story (*when I could break out from being a decent leg on a relay…*)?

A Definition 1

B Definition 2

C Definition 3

D Definition 4

USE "A FIRE CAPTAIN'S EULOGY" (pp. 24-250) to answer questions 15–28.

15 In paragraph 8, Captain Gormley contrasts the way we feel when a friend or a brother dies with the way we feel when a comrade dies. Which of his words tell us what is special or unique about the latter?

A *We are proud to have known a better man than ourselves.*

B *We grieve the future without them.*

C *We regret words unspoken.*

D *We remember the love.*

16 Which of the following quotations expresses a theme of the selection?

A *It's harder to be a comrade than a friend. They need you to be better.*

B *The depth and broadness of Frank's historical knowledge was astounding.*

C *We never went for a hike in the Shawangunk Mountains together.*

D *You can take your ease with [friends and brothers]—tell them tall tales.*

17 According to the selection, the main difference between comrades and friends is that —

A comrades are more jovial than friends

B comrades depend on each other absolutely

C you can forgive things in a comrade that you cannot in a friend.

D you can share laughter and tall tales with comrades

18 In paragraph 12, what does Frank's "look" express?

A a sense of humor and fun

B appreciation and thanks

C bewilderment and lack of understanding

D rough dismissal of sentimentality applied to himself

19 What is one reason that Captain Gormley felt it was appropriate that he delivered his eulogy in the Lincoln Center for Performing Arts?

A Captain Frank Callahan was a trusted leader.

B Lincoln Center is an easy place to get to.

C Lincoln himself was a great president and a true comrade.

D Throughout history, the arts have always helped mankind to deal with reality.

20 Which quotation from the selection best illustrates the responsibilities of captains in the Fire Department?

A Captains, especially commanding officers of companies in the same quarters, have a unique relationship.

B We go first. If things go badly, we are required by our oath and tradition to be the last of our command to leave.

C We know each other as no one else ever will.

D When we meet for the first time we introduce ourselves to each other, we shake hands.

21 In paragraph 21 Captain Gormley says, "We both believed captain to be the most important rank in the department." What is the most probable reason for his statement?

A Captains are the highest-paid firefighters in the fire department.

B Captains must both lead their men and possess firefighting skills.

C Once you are a captain, you have excellent opportunities for promotion and moving up in the department hierarchy.

D The reports filed by captains will help determine how department work is carried out.

22 In a metaphor in paragraph 23, Captain Gormley calls Captain Callahan "a star." What characteristic of a star does he use in this comparison?

A Stars are very far away.

B Stars look wonderful and mysterious.

C Stars may have planets revolving around them.

D You can find your compass direction from a star.

23 Read the following dictionary entry:

temper (tem' per), **1:** proneness to anger   **2:** to harden steel by heating it and cooling it in oil   **3:** to make stronger through hardship   **4:** to adjust the pitch of a note

Which definition best matches the meaning of the word *tempered* as it is used in paragraph 21 of the story?

A   Definition 1

B   Definition 2

C   Definition 3

D   Definition 4

24 In paragraph 1, Captain Gormley says, *Our aggressiveness is based on the trust we share in each other*. What does he mean by this?

A   Firefighting is a dangerous job, and we have to be aggressive.

B   We act belligerent, but we know it's all for show.

C   We can rush into danger because we have confidence in the men who are beside us.

D   We fight a lot, but we don't really mean it.

25 In paragraph 22, Captain Gormley says of Captain Callahan, *If more of the world's leaders were forged as he was, our world would not be in its current shape*. Which characteristics of Captain Callahan led Captain Gormley to say this?

A   his fondness for hiking in the mountains.

B   his integrity and his record of fearless leadership

C   his sense of humor and fondness for a practical joke

D   the depth of his historical knowledge

26 Paragraph 17 says that when the firefighters put on their protective gear, they also wrote their name or their Social Security number on their arm or leg. Why did they do this?

A   It's a good luck custom of the Fire Department.

B   It's a way, in times of danger, of assuring themselves who they are.

C   The Social Security Act requires firefighters to do this.

D   They do it so that they can be identified in case of disaster.

27 In paragraph 2, which word helps the reader understand the meaning of the word *accountability*?

A   carved

B   command

C   responsibility

D   tradition

28 What does paragraph 16 tell us about the conversations between the two captains?

A   They avoided serious discussion of controversial topics.

B   They were about ordinary, daily events.

C   They were often grim and filled with foreboding.

D   They were short and to the point.

USE "THE RACE" AND "A FIRE CAPTAIN'S EULOGY"
to answer questions 29 and 30.

---

29 How might you compare or contrast
the friends in the two selections?

A The fire captains and José and
Danny are all deeply involved in
sports.

B The fire captains are about the
same age; José and Danny are not.

C The fire captains have no lives
outside of their jobs, which José
and Danny do.

D The two fire captains probably felt
the same way about each other;
José and Danny don't.

30 What is the most important difference
between the nature of the friendships
in the two selections?

A One is about sports; the other is
about firefighting.

B One is based on rivalry, the other
on comradeship.

C One is during high school; the
other is long after high school.

D One is fictional; the other is
factual.

USE THE VISUAL REPRESENTATION ON PAGE 243
to answer questions 31 and 32.

---

31 The motto of the Student Council is —

A "Meet Your Study Buddy"

B "Need a better way to get help?"

C "Scared you might not graduate?"

D "Students helping Students"

32 The main message of this bulletin
board posting is meant for —

A 10th grade students having
trouble with their courses

B members of the Student Council

C students who use the library

D students who want to run for
Student Council

OPEN-ENDED ITEMS

33 A possible alternative title for "The Race" is "Breaking Away." Explain why this alternative title fits the story. Support your answer with evidence from the selection.

_____

_____

_____

_____

34 In "A Fire Captain's Eulogy," how did Captain James Gormley's experiences shape the way he felt about Captain Frank Callahan? Support your answer with evidence from the selection.

_____

_____

_____

_____

35 Both José and Captain Callahan faced tests of loyalty—José to Danny, the Captain to the men of his command. How well did each one pass or fail the test? Support your answer with evidence from the selection.

_____

_____

_____

_____

WRITTEN COMPOSITION

Write a composition explaining the importance and difficulty of maintaining friendships in your life.

The information in the box below will help you remember what you should think about when you write your composition.

REMEMBER—YOU SHOULD

- **write about the assigned topic**

- **make your writing thoughtful and interesting**

- **make sure that each sentence you write contributes to the composition as a whole**

- **make sure that your ideas are clear and easy for the reader to follow**

- **write about your ideas in depth so that the reader is able to develop a good understanding of what you are**

- **proofread your writing to correct errors in spelling, capitalization, punctuation, grammar, and sentence structure**

Revising and Editing—Selection 1

Robert and Louisa wrote the following letter to the Board of Trustees for the Austin Independent School District. Help them make the letter more persuasive by reading it over and answering the questions that follow.

[1] We understand that you are thinking about having a dress code for the Austin Independent School District so that students would dress properly. [2] We heard Dr. Nevarrez speak at the board of trustees meeting about both the pros and cons, an expert on dress codes, and we have some thoughts we'd like to share with you.

[3] As Dr. Nevarrez pointed out, a dress code usually restricts you're choice of clothing in some way. [4] For example, with a dress code you can't wear T-shirts that advertise alcohol or tobacco. [5] Also, you can't get your hair cut in certain ways or wear just any kind of shoes. [6] The dress code makes sure that everyone look neat and respectful.

[7] In her speech, Dr. Nevarrez said that one of the good points about having a dress code is that people respect you when you dress properly. [8] If you wear anything you want. [9] People don't think you're serious about school. [10] When you go to a party, you dress up for it. [11] When you go to a job interview, you dress properly, too. [12] You look like you mean to be there, and everyone treats you that way. [13] According to Dr. Nevarrez, there is even research that shows that students generally do better in school when there is a dress code.

[14] Another good point that Dr. Nevarrez mentioned is that you can save money for your family by not wanting something different to wear all the time. [15] When you're not dressing in the latest fad, you don't need as many clothes. [16] Students can also save money by not going to as many movies.

[17] Dr. Nevarrez pointed out that restricting your choice of clothing might not always be a good thing. [18] What about the very hot days we often have here in Austin? [19] If the dress code says that you ca'nt wear shorts, many students will be uncomfortable many days during the school year. [20] When you are uncomfortable, you can't concentrate, and your schoolwork might suffer.

[21] Another point that Dr. Nevarrez mentioned is that individuality in clothing might

be a harmless way for teenagers to express themselves. [22] This might be especially important for high school students. [23] If they feel too restricted by the dress code, they might find destructive ways to rebel.

[24] We hope you will think carefully about both sides of this issue before you decide whether a dress code is a good idea for the Austin Independent School District. [25] Will dressing seriously help us be more serious in school, or will it just make us feel uncomfortable.

---

1 What is the most effective way to rewrite sentence 2?

A We heard an expert on dress codes Dr. Nevarrez, speak at the board of trustees meeting and we have some thoughts, about both the pros and cons we'd like to share with you.

B We have some thoughts about both the pros and cons we'd like to share with Dr. Nevarrez, an expert on dress codes, and we can speak at the board of trustees meeting.

C We heard Dr. Nevarrez, an expert on dress codes, speak at the board of trustees meeting about both the pros and cons, and we have some thoughts we'd like to share with you.

D We heard both the pros and cons of dress codes at the board of trustees meeting, and Dr. Nevarrez has some thoughts we'd like to share with you.

2 What change, if any, should be made in sentence 3?

A Delete the comma after *out*

B Change *you're* to **your**

C Change *some way* to **way's**

D Make no change

3 What change, if any, should be made in sentence 6?

A Change *code* to **coad**

B Delete the word **that**

C Change *look* to **looks**

D Make no change

4 What is the most effective way to rewrite the ideas in sentences 8 and 9?

A If you wear anything you want, people won't think you're serious about school.

B If you wear anything you want; people don't think you're serious about school.

C People don't think if you wear anything you want you're serious about school.

D If you're serious about school, you don't wear anything people want.

5 What change, if any, should be made in sentence 11?

A Delete the word *a*

B Delete the comma after *interview*

C Change *too* to **to**

D Make no change

6 What is the most effective way to improve the organization of the fourth paragraph (sentences 14–16)?

    A Move sentence 15 to the beginning of the paragraph

    B Move sentence 15 to the end of the paragraph

    C Move sentence 16 to the beginning of the paragraph

    D Delete sentence 16

7 What transition should be added to the beginning of sentence 17?

    A On the other hand,

    B Therefore,

    C Moreover,

    D Meanwhile,

8 What change should be made in sentence 19?

    A Change *says* to **say**

    B Change *ca'nt* to **can't**

    C Change the comma after *shorts* to a semicolon

    D Change *schoolwork* to **school work**

9 The meaning of sentence 22 can be clarified by changing ***This*** to —

    A This harmlessness

    B This self expression

    C Their clothes

    D Themselves

10 What change should be made in sentence 25?

    A Change ***dressing seriously*** to **dress serious**

    B Change ***serious*** to **seriously**

    C Change the comma after ***school*** to a semicolon

    D Change the period to a question mark

Revising and Editing— Selection 2

Belinda wrote the essay below for a class on citizenship. To make her argument more convincing, read Belinda's essay carefully and answer the questions that follow it.

[1] Volunteer work can be very rewarding. [2] I am in favor of requiring all high school students to do 100 hours of community service in order to graduate. [3] You can learn a great deal from volunteer work. [4] For example, you can learn how to keep track of expenses on a project or how to teach someone a skill. [5] In addition, its important to learn the value of volunteer work so that people will go on volunteering. [6] There are many organizations that are dependent on volunteers.

[7] Students may complain that 100 hours is a lot of time, but over the course of four years it's nothing. [8] Even if you limit community service to 11th and 12th grades. [9] That's only a little over an hour a week during the school year. [10] Those hundred hours take very little of you're time, but they mean a lot to the people you help. [11] In 100 hours you can read a lot of stories to little kids or bring a lot of meals to elderly people.

[12] In my volunteer jobs, Ive learned something about teaching. [13] I've learned how to take care of babies. [14] Although I had some experience already taking care of my baby brother, I got even more. [15] I've learned about how a hospital is run. [16] And I've learned something even more important. [17] I now know how good it feels when you make someone else smile.

[18] When you help others you help yourself, too. [19] You learn things that you can't learn in school, you become an active part of your community. [20] If we want a better world in the new century, we need to incourage young people to become volunteers. [21] The best way to do this is to make it a graduation requirement.

[22] My classmates may grumble about my proposal. [23] Volunteering will make them better citizens, though. [24] It will also give all of us important skills. [25] When we leave high school three years from now, we will be better prepared to enter the world.

1   What is the most effective way to improve the organization of the first paragraph (sentences 1–6)?

    A   Move sentence 2 to the end of the paragraph

    B   Move sentence 3 to the end of the paragraph

    C   Move sentence 5 between sentences 1 and 2

    D   Move sentence 6 to the beginning of the paragraph

NOTICE: Photocopying any part of this book is forbidden by law.

255

2 What change should be made in sentence 5?

   A Delete the comma after *addition*

   B Change *its* to **it's**

   C Insert a comma after *work*

   D Change *volunteering* to **volunteered**

3 What is the most effective way to rewrite the ideas in sentences 8 and 9?

   A That's only a little over an hour in the 11th and 12th grades, even if you limit community service to a week during the school year.

   B That's only during the school year, even if you limit community service to 11th and 12th grades, a little over an hour a week.

   C Even if you limit community service to 11th and 12th grades; that's only a little over an hour a week during the school year.

   D Even if you limit community service to 11th and 12th grades, that's only a little over an hour a week during the school year.

4 What change should be made in sentence 10?

   A Change *Those* to **These**

   B Change *you're* to **your**

   C Delete the comma after *time*

   D Change *help* to **helped**

5 What change, if any, should be made in sentence 12?

   A Delete the comma after *jobs*

   B Change *Ive* to **I've**

   C Change *something* to **some**

   D Make no change

6 Which transition could be added to the beginning of sentence 15?

   A In addition,

   B Therefore,

   C Then

   D Sometimes,

7 What change, if any, should be made in sentence 18?

   A Insert a comma after *others*

   B Delete the comma after *yourself*

   C Change *too* to **to**

   D Make no change

8 What change should be made in sentence 19?

   A Change *learn* to **learned**

   B Change *can't* to **ca'nt**

   C Change the comma after *school* to a semicolon

   D Change *become* to **have become**

9 What change, if any, should be made in sentence 20?

   A Change *century* to **Century**

   B Change the comma after *century* to a semicolon

   C Change *incourage* to **encourage**

   D Make no change

10 The meaning of sentence 21 can be clarified by changing *it* to —

   A that

   B this

   C a better world

   D 100 hours of volunteer work